Series / Number 07-040

MICROCOMPUTER METHODS FOR SOCIAL SCIENTISTS

SECOND EDITION

PHILIP A. SCHRODT
Northwestern University

SAGE PUBLICATIONS
The Publishers of Professional Social Science
Newbury Park   Beverly Hills   London   New Delhi

For information address:

SAGE Publications, Inc.
2111 West Hillcrest Drive
Newbury Park, California 91320

SAGE Publications Inc.
275 South Beverly Drive
Beverly Hills
California 90212

SAGE Publications Ltd.
28 Banner Street
London EC1Y 8QE
England

SAGE PUBLICATIONS India Pvt. Ltd.
M-32 Market
Greater Kailash I
New Delhi 110 048 India

International Standard Book Number 0-8039-3043-7

Library of Congress Catalog Card No. 86-060131

FIRST PRINTING, 1987

When citing a university paper, please use the proper form. Remember to cite the correct
Sage University Paper series title and include the paper number. One of the following
formats can be adapted (depending on the style manual used):

(1) IVERSEN, GUDMUND R. and NORPOTH, HELMUT (1976) "Analysis of
Variance." Sage University Paper series on Quantitative Applications in the Social
Sciences, 07-001. Beverly Hills: Sage Pubns.

OR

(2) Iversen, Gudmund R. and Norpoth, Helmut. 1976. *Analysis of Variance.* Sage
University Paper series on Quantitative Applications in the Social Sciences, series no.
07-001. Beverly Hills: Sage Pubns.

CONTENTS

Preface to the Second Edition

The first edition of *Microcomputer Methods for Social Scientists* was written in the fall of 1983; this revision is being written almost exactly three years later. Those three years have seen a variety of changes and, even more, stabilization in the microcomputer field, all of which made for substantial changes in the book.

In hardware, the most important changes are the success of the Apple Macintosh, with its visually oriented operating system, and the clear hegemony of the IBM-PC/MS-DOS standard in the non-Apple market, all but eliminating the CP/M machines. For the social scientist, the greatest change in these three years has been the availability of mainframe-quality statistical packages, including SPSS. In programming, Borland International rescued Pascal from the obscurity to which it would have fallen in the hands of SofTech; the structured languages Pascal and C now clearly dominate microcomputer programming. Other applications that did not exist in 1983 have become common: desktop publishing, graphics editing (e.g., MacPaint), and RAM-resident utilities.

About half of the book has been extensively revised. Chapter 6 (covering statistics) was totally rewritten to emphasize commercial packages rather than programming. The old Chapter 7 on data bases was eliminated and replaced with a general chapter on software. Chapter 9 contains a new section on repairs. Chapter 3 (on operating systems) remains the same in structure but now discusses the Macintosh OS and UNIX instead of CP/M, the UCSD p-System, and Apple DOS; MS-DOS alone remains. Chapters 1, 2 (hardware), 4 (word processing), 5 (programming), 8 (graphics), and 10 (final thoughts) were updated to reflect new equipment and software trends. Throughout the book I have included many more references to specific software, because the long-term players in this game are now more obvious.

I anticipate revising this book every three or four years, depending on sales. As such, suggestions on topics that should be added or eliminated would be appreciated. My address is Department of Political Science, Northwestern University, Evanston, IL 60201.

MICROCOMPUTER METHODS FOR SOCIAL SCIENTISTS

SECOND EDITION

PHILIP A. SCHRODT
Northwestern University

1. INTRODUCTION

Purpose

Predictions of the microcomputer's long-term impact on the social sciences evoke the observation of J.B.S. Haldane: "The universe is not only stranger than we imagine, it is stranger than we *can* imagine." A microcomputer provides the individual social scientist with resources for information access, manuscript preparation, simulation, statistical analysis and graphics design that were available only to heavily funded research teams twenty years ago, and available to no one fifty years ago.

Between the present and the computerized future, however, lies a dense thicket of media hype, obscure jargon, incomplete information, and general uncertainty about microcomputers. Coherent information on microcomputers is scarce even in the popular realm of business applications, and nearly nonexistent in many academic applications, which are perceived as an amusing sideline by many hardware and software manufacturers. What a computer can and cannot do is unclear, information sources are limited, and the technology often *appears* to be changing so rapidly that full-time study is required to stay current.

Against that background, this book is intended to meet three needs. First, it is a basic introduction to the terminology and use of microcomputers. Second, it is a guide to how to *learn* about microcomputers and microcomputer software. Third, it surveys many applications of micros in a social science context.

The text deals with features common to most microcomputers, and surveys common hardware and software. Emphasis is placed on avoiding common mistakes such as substituting "O" for "zero" or leaving a floppy disk on the radiator. Programs common to all microcomputers—operating systems, editors, programming languages, graphics, and communications—are discussed in detail, and some specialized applications are discussed briefly. This provides some sense of the tasks for which a microcomputer is appropriate.

Learning how to learn about microcomputers is treated here because, during the course of a career, any professional will use at least a half-dozen different computer systems, whether through job changes or technology changes. Learning each new system can be simple or difficult, depending on how the task is approached. Each system will differ in its particulars, but each will be similar in what it can do.

Learning how to learn involves recognition of the small set of computer functions that account for most of the work. Computers are used primarily to store and retrieve information, edit and format text, perform standard mathematical routines, communicate with other computers, and prepare graphics. In ten years computers will still spend 90 percent of their time doing these tasks, albeit more quickly, more conveniently, and with different commands. The key is recognizing those functions.

This book is directed toward the needs and skills of the social science community—both students and professionals—as distinct from the business, home, natural science or industrial community. While brevity of the monograph format precludes many direct social science examples—and much of the content applies to any microcomputer user—I have emphasized those applications most relevant to social scientists. Thus, little space is devoted to spreadsheets, a staple business application, and considerable space is given to statistics and programming.

Scope and Terminology

This book focuses on the "personal computer" (PC), defined as a desk-top computer typified by the IBM personal computer series (IBM PC, XT, and AT) and the numerous IBM-compatible "clones," and computers with visually oriented operating systems (VOS) such as the Apple Macintosh, Atari ST series, and the Commodore Amiga. These machines have at least 256K of memory, usually two disk drives, peripheral connections to handle telecommunications and hard disks, access to a printer, and a large software base; they cost about $1,000-$2,500.

The term *older computers* will refer to older business-oriented PCs, such as the Osborne and Kaypro transportables and some configurations of the Apple II series. These machines had more limited memory (usually 64K) and more primitive operating systems than the current generation of PCs. While little new software is being written for these machines, millions are still in use and they function perfectly well as word processors. There are microcomputers even older than these, dating back to the middle 1970s, but they are rarely encountered.

The term *work station* refers to "super-micros," usually found in specialized graphics and artificial intelligence applications. These usually have high-speed processors, hard disks, multiple megabytes of memory, and high-resolution graphics displays, and use either UNIX or visually oriented operating systems. Such machines cost anywhere from $10,000 to $50,000 and are rarely found in the social science environment.

Prices are circa fall 1986 and will change over time. Prices vary substantially depending on the quality and capabilities of equipment, and discounting arrangements. For current price information consult *Byte, InfoWorld, Personal Computing,* and other microcomputer publications. The speed and capability limitations are also approximate and somewhat conservative.

Microcomputers can be configured with various hardware and software depending on the intended application. A microcomputer equipped with all of the hardware and software described here would cost around $30,000, and mastery of the system would take years. In the text I will try to distinguish between the basic hardware and software—such as editors, operating systems, and printers—and hardware and software likely to be encountered only in specialized applications.

Computer professionals employ a large specialized vocabulary in discussing various functions and features of machines. Since knowledge of this vocabulary is necessary for reading current periodicals and books, I will introduce and use a number of unfamiliar words. This section will introduce a few of those terms; others will be introduced in later chapters.

Mainframe—a large, fast, multiple-user computer typical of a university computer center.

Microcomputer—a computer small enough to fit easily on a desk, usually designed for a single user.

I/O—input-output, as in "Disk I/O," information written to and read from a disk.

File—a set of information stored on a disk. Disk storage is divided into files, which are in turn used by programs. An example of a file would be a document for word processing, or a set of data for a statistics program.

Software—programs. Most software is produced and purchased separately from the PC.

Operating system—a program that controls the overall operations of the machine and performs such functions as allocating memory, running programs and operating the disks.

Resolution—the amount of detail a screen or printer can show. High resolution indicates more detail than low resolution.

Byte—the basic unit of storage in a microcomputer, equivalent to one alphanumeric character or a number between 0 and 255. A byte is eight "bits"; a bit is either one or zero.

K—1024, which is 2 to the tenth power. Used as a unit of measure of memory capacity; e.g., a 64K memory contains 64 times 1024 or 65,536 bytes.

Chip—integrated circuit chip, the basic electronic component of a PC. A chip is a tiny piece of etched silicon embedded in a plastic carrier with wire leads. "Chip" is used to refer to parts of the computer, e.g. memory chips, microprocessor chips.

Considerable additional vocabulary and jargon will be introduced in later chapters. I will confine the jargon to that in common use, but there is a lot of it.

What Microcomputers Can and Cannot Do

A PC can:

- Act as a word processor with extensive text editing and formatting capabilities. With supplemental programs it can check spelling and style, manage mailing lists and form letters, and format footnotes and bibliographies. Software: $50-$500 (Chapter 4).

- Maintain and intelligently access 500-2000 data records, depending on record size, with sorting, updating, and selection on the data base. Software: $100-$800. With a "hard disk" ($1000-$3000) much larger files can be maintained (Chapter 7).

- Do almost any statistical analysis on data sets up to a sample size of at least 2000 for 20 to 40 variables. With a hard disk, the data set can be much larger. For large data sets a PC will be noticeably slower than a time-shared mainframe; for small sets it will be faster. Software: $400-$1,500 (Chapter 6).

- Be programmed in most any computer programming language, including BASIC, Pascal, assembly language, FORTRAN, LISP, Prolog, C, Ada, APL, and many others. Software: $0-$500 (Chapter 5).

- Function as a remote terminal and transfer files to and from other computers, including mainframes. Software: $50-$200; hardware: $100-$500. With proper software, a PC can emulate intelligent terminals such as the DEC VT100 or Tektronix graphics terminals (Chapter 9).

- Handle moderately large mathematical simulations and numerical problems at roughly one-tenth the speed of a mainframe (Chapter 6).

- Produce statistical graphics and other graphics material with a resolution of around 400 by 300 points per display. Graphics can be printed on a dot-matrix printer—software: $30-$100—or plotter—$1,000-$2,000 (Chapter 8).

- Monitor and operate laboratory equipment and physical devices. Interface: $100-$300 (Chapter 9).
- "Speak" using a synthesizer. Music can also be synthesized. Hardware: $300-$1,000 (Chapter 9).
- "See" in black and white using a solid-state camera. Hardware: $300-$1000 (Chapter 8).

A PC cannot:

- Do anything that it has not been told to do in a program. Software is expensive and must be purchased or written.
- Understand speech. Hardware for speech input is available, but the software is experimental and unpredictable.
- See color, see detail, or display gray tones without special equipment. Graphics are confined to black and white on most machines, and most cameras are fairly primitive.
- Read printed or handwritten text. PC peripherals for this are experimental and expensive.
- Manipulate objects using a robot arm or drive a robot. Few PC robot peripherals are available, and their capabilities are very limited.

Organization of the Book

Introduction—This describes what a particular function or application of a PC is and does, and acquaints you with some vocabulary; it is the most elementary level of discussion.

Operation—This discusses how to learn to use, or how to evaluate, a microcomputer application (e.g., word processing, statistics, programming), and will be easiest to follow if you are actually using a microcomputer.

Advanced—This material goes beyond the basic operation, and consists of suggestions on how to extend the use of the PC after you have mastered the basic elements. The Advanced section presupposes some acquaintance with the basic operation and can be skipped if you are interested only in an introduction.

Troubleshooting—This deals with the most common errors encountered in each application; it is designed to provide suggestions of what to check when the machine doesn't work correctly.

The most important single step in learning to use a computer is to let it teach you. Make mistakes, experiment, try a dozen things to find out what works; don't get frustrated when something doesn't work the first time. The machine's time and patience are less valuable than your time and patience. If you have to switch the machine off a few times, or use RESET, don't worry. Failure is the road to success.

Eventually you will reach a point at which the system works so smoothly you'll wonder why you ever had problems. You will accumulate a set of tricks that work for you (though not necessarily anybody else) and a set of work habits that make the machine an extension of your mind in the same way a hand tool is an extension of the body. But this takes some time and practice, and don't get discouraged in the meantime.

My suggestions on learning to learn and troubleshooting are based on a combination of common sense, hindsight and twelve years of teaching computer programming and the use of computers. The statement "I do X" means I've been doing something (e.g., spraying WD-40 on printer ribbons) sufficiently long that if it was going to cause problems, it would have, and hasn't. Such practices may not be officially recommended. Follow the advice at your own risk. Because of the seemingly infinite creativity exhibited by users (including myself) in discovering new and unusual ways of causing computers to malfunction, the troubleshooting hints will not solve all problems, but they are a start.

I have attempted to be technically accurate in examples whenever possible. However, operating systems and machine configurations evolve over time, so the examples may not apply to the machine you are using. This book is not a substitute for an operating system or PC reference manual, only a guide to it.

2. HARDWARE

This chapter will discuss the physical components of the microcomputer, their functions, and how to use them properly. It will also survey some common computer accessories.

The physical structure of a microcomputer is shown schematically in Figure 2.1. Conveniently, the physical structure of a microcomputer corresponds to a great extent to its logical structure. The central processing unit (CPU) is the heart and brain of the computer and controls the other functions. The CPU has access to memory, which can be either read and written as temporary storage (random-access memory or RAM) or which is permanent and contains commonly used programs (read-only memory or ROM). These parts of the computer are silicon chips and reside on the "motherboard" of the computer.

The CPU communicates with the outside world using a variety of devices. A typewriterlike keyboard receives input and a televisionlike CRT displays output. For storage of information outside of memory, the PC uses disk drives, which read and write magnetic disks. A printer is used for permanent copies of text and graphics. In addition, a wide variety of accessory "peripherals" (such as modems, plotters, speech synthesizers, video cameras) can be attached to the computer through interfaces.

Introduction: Physical Components

The microcomputer consists of five main parts: motherboard, keyboard, CRT, disk drives, and peripherals.

MOTHERBOARD

The motherboard is the central part of the computer and contains the microprocessor, memory, chips for coordinating memory and I/O, a power supply, and connection slots for peripheral interfaces. The motherboard is housed inside the PC's cabinet, unseen unless the cabinet cover is removed.

A microprocessor is the central control for the machine. It contains the CPU, which performs the arithmetic and logical functions, and an

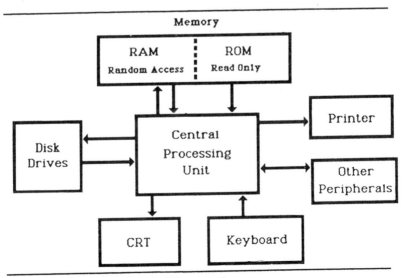

Figure 2.1 Physical Structure of a Microcomputer

assortment of memory and I/O controllers. While many microprocessors exist, only a few are in wide use:

- Z-80 family—a series of chips used in most early PCs. The original CP/M operating system worked with this chip.
- Intel 8000 family—a series of chips used in the IBM PC family, including the 8088, 8086, 80286, and 80386. MS-DOS in almost universally used as the operating system in Intel systems.
- Motorola 68000 family—used in most machines with visually oriented operating systems (e.g., Apple Macintosh; Atari ST series); the 68020 is its more powerful successor, long used in work stations and now beginning to appear in PCs.

Generally software written for one microprocessor will not run unchanged on a different microprocessor; for example, an Apple Macintosh with a 68000 processor cannot run MS-DOS software, which requires an Intel microprocessor. However, a PC can have more than one microprocessor by using a "coprocessor"—a second microprocessor, which takes over from the original. With appropriate coprocessors, an IBM can run Apple software or an Apple can run IBM or CP/M software.

Random-access memory (RAM) is read/write memory, which can be changed by programs; it is erased when the machine is turned off. Read-only memory (ROM) is permanent and usually contains instructions to start running the computer when it is first turned on. Memory is measured in kilobytes, or K. While in theory a 64K memory could hold 65,536 characters, or about 30 typewritten pages, the memory must hold the operating instructions for the computer as well as any programs, so the memory available to a program is less than the total memory.

The "power supply" of the computer is a fairly large, sealed, metal box. It harbors potentially fatal voltages even when the machine is not plugged in. Leave it alone.

"Slots" on the motherboard hold interface cards for peripherals, which are discussed below.

KEYBOARD

The keyboard of a PC looks and functions like an electric typewriter keyboard, except that it has a number of additional keys—frequently quite a number. Unlike a typewriter, the function of most of the keys is controlled by the software rather than fixed, so the same key may do different things in different programs. While different PCs have various special keys, the following are common:

RETURN (or Enter)—This key sends a typed line of information to the CPU; it is effectively a "transmit."

CTRL (or ALT)—The "control" key modifies the values of other keys. It is used widely in word processing programs. To use the CTRL key, hold it down while *simultaneously* typing the other letter. These commands are usually abbreviated with the notation CTRL-C (pronounced "control C"), CTRL-S, and so forth; the notation ∧S is also used. An ALT key may exist in place of, or in addition to, the CTRL key; it has a similar function. (Be careful to avoid using CTRL characters where they don't belong, as these may have unpredictable effects on your machine and/or printer. For example, CTRL-S causes many PCs to stop functioning. On some terminals control characters erase lines or otherwise act unexpectedly, which complicates editing.)

ESC—The "escape" key does not have a standard use but tends to interrupt or cancel program functions. Avoid hitting it accidentally.

Cursor controls—The cursor is a line or box, usually blinking, which indicates where typed characters will appear on the screen. Somewhere on the keyboard are keys to move it, usually with little arrows on them. The key with the arrow pointing left serves as a backspace; for historical reasons, CTRL-H usually backspaces as well. Many machines have keys for clearing the screen, displaying a new page of text, and other screen control functions.

Function keys—These consist of a series of large keys usually located above the top row of keys or along the side, and tend to be labeled either F1, F2, etc., or P1, P2, etc. They are "programmable function keys," and their use depends entirely on software; they will frequently do nothing at all.

RESET—This is a switch or key usually located off the keyboard, sometimes on the back of the machine, but generally where it cannot be pressed accidentally. Pressing RESET allows recovery from most error conditions, at the expense of having to restart the program and losing anything in memory. Use it with caution. On many machines it is necessary to press several keys simultaneously to reset.

Numeric keypad—Many keyboards have a 4 × 4 set of keys that can be used for entering numbers. These may also serve as an alternative cursor control.

Generally there is nothing difficult about using a PC keyboard, though if you are a skilled touch typist the extra keys and the imaginative keyboard layout employed on some machines may cause problems at first. Most PCs have an "auto-repeat" feature, which causes keys to repeat automatically when they are held down for more than a couple of seconds.

CRT

The video screen is called a CRT (cathode ray tube), VDU (video display unit), or simply "monitor" or "screen." It is essentially a high-resolution closed-circuit television set. The important controls are brightness and contrast; usually these are adjusted with knobs on the set. CRTs usually have a green or amber tint; color monitors are good for graphics but usually poor for word processing because of low resolution.

Proper adjustment of a CRT is important when it is used for an extended time. Adjustment includes setting the correct contrast and brightness, finding a comfortable angle of viewing, and adjusting room lighting to reduce reflections. An improperly adjusted CRT will cause headaches and stress from eyestrain.

DISK DRIVES AND FLOPPY DISKS

This is the least familiar, and most critical, part of a PC. The "floppy disk" was a key element in the development of the PC, since it enabled the computer to access and save a large amount of information quickly. The disk storage capacity is usually five to ten times the capacity of RAM.

Disks come in three common sizes: 3.5-inch (88 mm) disks have a hard plastic shell and are standard on many newer machines; 5¼-inch (13 cm) disks are encased in a flexible plastic envelope and are used in virtually every PC introduced between 1980 and 1985, including most IBM-compatible PCs; and some older PCs used 8-inch (20 cm) disks, though these are now uncommon. Contrary to intuition, the physical size of a disk bears little relationship to the amount of information it holds: Some 3.5-inch disks hold more than some 8-inch disks. All of these disks are called "floppy" despite the fact that 3.5-inch disks aren't at all flexible; the word *floppy* distinguishes them from fixed, high-capacity, hard disks.

Disks must be suitable for the PC in which they are used. Disk drives with high storage densities—"double-density" or "quad-density" drives—cannot use older, single-density disks, or cheaper disks. Some systems require "hard-sectored" disks, which have holes punched near the inside rim for timing purposes. Disks cost between $2 and $5 each, but at any cost are cheap compared to the amount of effort required to replace information if the disk proves inadequate. Considerable money can be saved by buying disks by mail order and in bulk; brand names are significant since the quality varies with the manufacturer.

Disks written under one operating system usually cannot be read by a machine using a different operating system, even though the disks are physically identical. Thus even though some IBM-compatible computers can read and write 3.5-inch disks, those disks cannot be read by a standard Apple Macintosh, which uses a different format. Disks should be interchangeable between machines of the same type; if they are not, the speed of one of the disk drives probably needs adjustment.

The top side of a disk has a printed label. Information is recorded on the bottom side, so take particular care with that side. A "write-protect notch" is cut on the left side of the disk; if this notch is covered the disk can only be read, and not rewritten or erased, which protects against accidental erasure. On "double-sided disks" both sides of the disk are used to store information, and there are two write-protect notches. When inserting a disk in a drive, *be gentle.* If the disk jams, don't try to force it, as the disk or drive might be damaged; get help in removing the disk.

With proper care, floppy disks are very reliable. But proper care is required. Twenty hours of work can be destroyed by a second of carelessness. The recording surface of a disk is very thinly coated with a magnetic substance similar to that used on recording tape. Information is stored by magnetizing or demagnetizing areas on the disk. A typical floppy disk has some 2.5 million magnetic bits on an area roughly 11 square inches (70 sq cm), or about 200,000 bits in the area of a postage stamp, so even a tiny amount of damage can affect a large amount of information. (Care of disks is described in detail under the troubleshooting section.)

Information on a disk should last a long time. Just how long is not clear—at least a year and probably a good deal longer. Ideally disks should be recopied every year or so to renew the magnetic fields if the disk is to be kept for a long period of time.

PRINTERS

Printers produce permanent copies of text and often graphics. The most common types of printer are the letter-quality printer and dot-matrix printer. Both use a conventional ink ribbon and ordinary paper, which may be continuous or in single sheets.

Impact printers work like a typewriter: Characters are formed by a hammer striking type against the ribbon causing an impression on the paper. Most letter-quality printers carry the type on a plastic or metal "daisy wheel," which spins and stops at the appropriate letter. Letter-quality printers produce documents that are indistinguishable from typewriting, and different typefaces can be obtained simply by switching type wheels. Letter-quality printers are somewhat slow, the type wheels and other moving parts break, they are poor for graphics, and they are expensive.

Dot-matrix printers form letters by striking the ribbon with several "needles" to form letters from a series of dots. On early dot matrix printers, the final result was distinctly inferior to a typewriter, though recent models come very close to typewriter quality, particularly after a document is photocopied. Dot matrix printers cost considerably less than letter-quality printers, are faster, contain fewer moving parts (thus are more reliable), are somewhat less noisy, can switch between type fonts under software control, and can be used to produce high-resolution graphics with appropriate software.

Laser printers are widely used in desktop publishing because they produce output almost indistinguishable from professional typesetting. A laser printer works on a principle similar to that of a photocopier: A low-power laser "writes" on a charged drum, which transfers an inklike toner to the paper. With appropriate software, laser printers can reproduce half-tone photographs as well as conventional computer-generated graphics. Laser printers are expensive—$2,000 to $5,000—but are dropping in price.

Printer ribbons need to be replaced periodically and it is useful to reserve a good ribbon for use only when printing final copies. Fabric ribbons can be rejuvenated by prying them open and spraying the ribbon with a solvent such as WD-40 (this procedure is not universally recommended), then waiting a day or two to allow the ink to diffuse from the unused to the worn areas of the ribbon. Reinking machines that will reink most fabric ribbons are available for $50-$80; these make the cost of reinking just a few cents per ribbon. The task is a bit messy but very cost-effective, particularly if the reinker is shared by several people.

Printer operation is discussed in detail in Chapter 4. Printers with continuous-feed paper *appear* to operate without attention. In actuality, they frequently jam, run out of paper, and otherwise need assistance. Until you have considerable experience with a printer, it is unwise to leave a printer running alone, even if others are doing so. On most printers I've used, a variation in paper placement of a quarter-inch (a few millimeters) may mean the difference between smooth flow and a jam.

Advanced: Peripherals

Technically speaking, a peripheral is anything that isn't actually on the motherboard, so in fact disk drives, the printer, and even the keyboard and CRT can be considered peripherals. The term is more commonly used to refer to any special accessories for the computer.

There is a small-scale industry devoted to developing and manufacturing peripherals for PCs, so a large number exist. A link is established between the peripheral and CPU using an interface circuit board, commonly called a "board" or "card." Boards plug into electrical contact slots on the motherboard and from there communicate with the CPU.

Increasingly, PCs are equipped with built-in interfaces. The most common interface is the RS-232C, a standard for "serial" communications between computers and peripherals such as printers, modems, and instruments. "Parallel" interfaces are frequently used with printers; the Centronix parallel is one standard. The Small Computer Standard Interface (SCSI, pronounced "scuzzy") peripheral connector is found on a number of newer computers and provides a standardized connection for high-speed peripherals such as hard disks. The word *port* is frequently used to refer to an interface connector, as in "scuzzy port."

This section will briefly describe some of the peripherals that might be attached to a computer. This is neither an exhaustive listing, nor is everything on this list a must for a well-equipped PC. Many of these items are discussed in more detail in later chapters.

Modem ($100-$500). A device used for communication between computers over phone lines. A modem usually employs a standard RS-232C serial interface and, hence, can also communicate with devices other than computers. "Intelligent" modems can automatically dial and log into other systems and transfer files.

Hard disk ($500-$3000). These are nonremovable disks that hold anywhere from 10 to 100 megabytes (1 megabyte = Mb = 1000K bytes) of information. They are considerably faster and more reliable than floppy disks, and are more convenient because a single hard disk will hold the contents of several boxes of floppies. Many 10 Mb and 20 Mb hard disks are small enough to fit on a card inside the computer or replace one of the floppy drives; larger hard disks usually sit outside the computer and connect through a peripheral port.

A new but potentially very useful technology is the "optical disk," which uses laser rather than magnetic storage techniques, and may provide storage for billions of bytes per disk. Optical disks promise to be more reliable and less fragile than magnetic disks and may evolve into the standard medium for very large files, such as census data or reference works.

Expansion RAM ($100-$500). Many machines can accept additional memory—anywhere from 16K to 4 Mb—in the form of cards installed in slots in the motherboard. This allows the memory of the machine to be expanded quite easily, since no changes to the motherboard itself are required. Expanded RAM will often make programs much easier to run, but not all programs are able to use expansion RAM. Standards are emerging, but check for software compatibility.

Print buffer ($200-$500). Printers are slow compared to the speed at which the CPU can transmit characters. A "buffer" of RAM placed between the computer and printer allows the CPU rapidly to transmit information to the memory, where it is released slowly to the printer. This frees the CPU for other tasks. Some operating systems do this with a programmed "spooler."

Coprocessors. A coprocessor is a microprocessor in a peripheral slot, which takes over most of the motherboard, in effect converting the PC to another computer. Coprocessors are used either to allow a machine to run software designed for another brand of computer or to increase speed by more efficiently performing certain tasks.

Graphics I/O. High-resolution screen graphics make up one of the most attractive features of PCs, but graphics input and output requires specialized peripherals. Input devices include graphics tablets, joysticks, and touch screens. Output devices include peripherals that increase screen resolution and color capabilities, graphics coprocessors, and plotters.

Voice I/O. Voice output of computers is very well developed: the effects are eerily natural, and programming is simple with the proper equipment. Voice recognition is still experimental and does not work easily, but hardware is available.

Analog-digital I/O. It is relatively simple and inexpensive to interface PCs to laboratory instruments and other devices that transmit or are controlled by voltages. This requires an A/D or D/A interface.

Troubleshooting: Environment

For its level of complexity, a microcomputer is a highly reliable device, and a far cry from the behemoths of the 1950s, which required a full-time cadre of technicians to replace their constantly failing parts. At the same time, an improper environment can reduce a $3000 PC to a functionless pile of plastic and silicon in short order. Since frequently the first sign of machine malfunction involves the destruction of two hours' work, the machine's environment is important. This section will deal with some common hazards.

Heat. The chips and power supply of a PC generate about as much heat as an incandescent light bulb. Additional peripheral cards, particularly RAM and graphics cards, will add significantly to this. The heat *must* be dissipated, and getting rid of the heat is complicated by the enclosed and crowded cabinet. Most PCs have fans, and those that do not, such as the Apple II, can be so equipped for $30-$100. Be sure that fans and cooling vents are not blocked by equipment, disks, or other items. A fan is useless if the air around the machine is warm. At Northwestern University our Apples encounter difficulties if the room temperature rises above 90 degrees F (32 C). The temperature in a room can increase substantially from sunlight or body heat unless the room has adequate ventilation.

When a machine is too warm, it functions erratically. On the Apple, for instance, the screen display and the disk drives are the first to go. When this happens, turn the machine off and allow it to cool. If a PC is severely overheated, permanent damage can result; in any case, you are likely to lose whatever you are doing, so quit while you are ahead. When running a machine for a very long period of time—overnight, for example—it is helpful to remove the cover to maximize air circulation, provided the machine is in a secure location.

Smoke and dust. Electronic devices are very sensitive to cigarette smoke, dust, and other small particles. A PC contains electrically charged areas, which attract inordinate amounts of tar from cigarettes, particularly on mechanical contacts. Since these contacts are the most fragile part of a PC, smoke accelerates the depreciation of the machine. If dust cannot be avoided, frequent cleaning, dust covers, and air filters are advisable.

Static electricity. On a dry winter day, tremendous levels of static electricity can build up on an individual, particularly in carpeted areas. These charges range into the thousands of volts and can destroy isolated integrated circuit chips.

Static discharge to an intact PC probably will not cause permanent damage, but often will sufficiently disrupt the CPU that the machine must be restarted, with the complete loss of memory.

To avoid static problems, always ground yourself to discharge static before touching the machine. Holding a set of keys in your palm and directing them at something grounded (NOT the computer!) is the least painful way of doing this. All parts of the PC should be grounded including detached peripherals such as disk drives, modems, and printers. This may involve running a wire from the peripheral to a grounding point on the machine. Antistatic mats prevent static buildup while one is using a machine.

Liquid. Computers and liquids—coffee, soft drinks, water, soup, ketchup, nail polish, beer—do not mix, and severe damage can result. Even tears have been known to short-circuit a keyboard. If liquid is spilled, shut off the machine immediately, then dry it. If the machine is perfectly dry when restarted, and no chemical deposits (e.g., sugar, coffee) remain, it should be okay unless damaged in the initial spill.

Unreliable power supplies. Microcomputers require a steady source of power. In most university environments this is not a problem, but PCs should be isolated from circuits that have sudden loads—e.g., the blowers for air conditioning systems. Erratic power is usually first evident from the CRT image, which will get dim, fuzzy, or otherwise weird. In such situations it is wise to shut off the machine and work on something else until the power becomes stable.

If erratic power is a problem, "voltage spike protection" circuits can be installed between the machine and the power line. These cost between $50 and $500, depending on speed and quality. "Uninterruptible power supplies" (UPS) that provide power for a sufficient time to save whatever programs were running on the machine are available ($400-$800) if power reliability is a major problem.

Wear and tear. The depreciation on a microcomputer is surprisingly low, but not zero. Moving parts such as the keyboard, printer, and disk drives are most likely to break after the initial "burn-in" of the electronic parts. Some "lemons" exist (we own one). If a machine is causing you inordinate amounts of trouble, try another. If you buy a PC, use it extensively while it is still under warranty. If *all* machines in a location have inordinate problems, the operating environment is probably at fault; check the heat, smoke, dust, power supply, and other factors.

Theft. Microcomputers have a tendency to get stolen. Software and peripherals are even more likely to get stolen. There are two solutions to this: Secure the machines (and particularly small, easily removed parts like boards and disks), and then insure the machines. If you own a PC, make sure your insurance policy covers PCs. Many standard policies do not and separate insurance must be purchased ($25-$75 for $5000 coverage). As a user, you may find these security arrangements inconvenient, but they are necessary.

Troubleshooting: Keyboard and Disks

The following are common keyboard errors:

- The letter O and the number 0 are not interchangeable.
- The lower-case letter l and the number 1 are not interchangeable.
- There are four different types of enclosures ( ), [ ], < >, and { }—they are frequently not interchangeable in programs.
- Distinguish between the underscore _ and the minus -.
- When touch typing, be careful to avoid hitting the CTRL, ESC, or ALT keys; striking one accidentally and hitting a letter simultaneously may have unpredictable results.
- Some older programs will respond only to input in upper case. If a program is not responding, press CAPS LOCK and try again.
- Distinguish between the SHIFT LOCK and CAPS LOCK keys. The latter shifts only on letters; the former shifts on all keys. Some machines also have a lock key that causes certain letters to act as a numeric keypad.

Disks will survive if you take the following precautions:

- Never touch the surface of the disk, and always leave the disk in the protective envelope except when it is in the drive. The oil in a fingerprint will disrupt the disk surface it touches.
- Use only felt tip pens to label disks, and use a light touch. Ballpoints and pencils destroy information by distorting the surface of the disk.
- Never expose disks to heat, for example, under hot lamps, on radiators, in direct sunlight, and in glove compartments. Even if the disk does not melt, heat will destroy the magnetic fields and distort the disk surface.
- Do not bend the disk. A disk will survive some bending but bending doesn't help. If a disk becomes bent, try copying it, then discard the original. Sometimes a bent disk can be saved by cutting open the jacket, transferring the disk into an unbent jacket, then copying it.
- Avoid magnetic fields! This, more than anything, is guaranteed, total, and sudden death for information recorded on the disk. No magnetic fields, eh? You'd be surprised where you will find them.

      —telephone bells
      —transformers in fluorescent desk lamps
      —motors in electric typewriters
      —color television sets
      —magnetic memo or paper clip holders

- Always make backup copies. If a disk is worth having, it's worth having a backup. This takes a little time, and another disk, but a $3 disk and five minutes is cheap insurance against losing 20 hours of work. Always back up everything—always.
- Use a "patch" program to recover information. While damage to only a small portion of a disk—particularly the disk directory—

can render it unreadable by a standard operating system, most of the information will still be intact. This can be recovered by a patch program, which attempts to read the disk and reconstruct the file despite the damage. Patch programs can usually recover text files even if they are partially damaged, and can recover data and program files if the file itself has not been damaged. These programs are relatively inexpensive ($25-$75) and pay for themselves the first time an important disk requires reconstructing.

3. OPERATING SYSTEMS

Introduction

The operating system (OS) is the master control program of a PC. It is responsible for reading and writing disks, running programs, managing information on disks, and general allocation of the machine's resources. Parts of the operating system function without the user being aware of them, but many features are directly accessible through operating system commands.

The logical structure of a microcomputer is shown schematically in Figure 3.1. The outermost level is the machine itself—the capabilities of the microprocessor, memory, disk drives, and peripherals. PCs have some fixed operating instructions in ROM that, at the very least, instruct the PC to read the disk containing the operating system when it is first turned on. Early microcomputers had *most* of their operating system in ROM, but newer PCs avoid ROM in order to keep the system reprogrammable, which simplifies upgrading the machine. The disk containing the operating system is called the "boot disk" (so called because the machine "pulls itself up by the bootstraps" as it reads in the disk) and the processing of reading in the OS is called "booting."

The operating system is the next level of control and is usually running after the machine is booted. In effect the boot disk wakes up the hardware and tells it what to do. In some applications the OS is invisible, since the boot instructions automatically run a program after loading the OS.

The OS has four primary functions. First, it governs the allocation of the resources of the machine, controlling the use of memory, reading the keyboard, sending output to the CRT or printer, and so forth. Second, the OS coordinates the activities of the CPU and the disk drives, for example, directing the CPU to run a program stored on disk. Third— and most important from the standpoint of the user—the OS maintains the disk files for the system. These files might contain text, programs, graphics, data, copies of memory, and other information. Finally, the OS provides utility programs to maintain disk directories, edit and copy files, execute command sequences automatically, and other functions.

Programs are under the control of the OS, though when a program is running, the OS operates in the background and may not be evident. Programs create and use their own data files, which may or may not be accessible later to the OS; and programs may be able to use files created by other programs, using the OS as an intermediary. It is always important to recognize whether the machine is on the SYSTEM level or the PROGRAM level, since different things can be done at different levels. A PC has many programs, but usually only one OS. The OS will work identically with all programs; the programs will operate differently.

It may seem needlessly confusing to have two separate levels of control. In fact, when microcomputers were first developed there was only one level, the program. As programs and machines became more complex, however, micros followed the pattern of mainframes and consolidated common program features such as the disk I/O into an OS. The programs operating within the OS thus did not need to provide these functions and, if properly designed, could share files.

A second advantage of operating systems is that different brands of PC can share the same OS, allowing users and programmers to switch between brands without learning a new system. The earliest common system, CP/M, is available on over 600 different models of microcomputer, enlarging the software base for all of them.

There are a number of operating systems, but the following are the most common:

CP/M (Digital Research)—The first common microcomputer OS, CP/M originally operated on machines using the Z-80 microprocessor. CP/M is no longer found on new machines but is still used in hundreds of thousands of older machines such as the Kaypro and Osbourne.

MS-DOS (MicroSoft)—MS-DOS is the operating system used on the IBM family of PCs and their associated clones. Many MS-DOS commands are similar to CP/M, though the internal structure of the system is quite different. It has gone through a number of revisions; the more recent versions have a huge set of functions and a hierarchical file structure.

UNIX—A complex OS originally developed for mainframes by Bell Laboratories; there are now two different "standards" and a variety of similar systems (e.g., XENIX, UNOS). UNIX is the first mainframe OS transplanted to micros. It makes massive demands on memory, speed, and storage, but is capable of far more sophisticated functions than other PC operating systems.

Visually Oriented Systems (VOS)—These are systems based on the pioneering work done at the Xerox Palo Alto Research Center (PARC). VOS use a hand-held "mouse" to manipulate pictures on the screen to execute com-

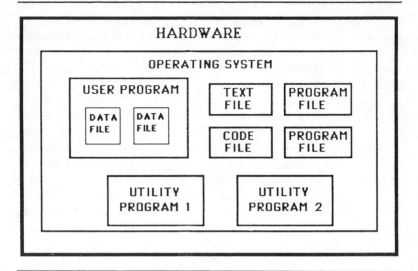

Figure 3.1 Logical Structure of a Microcomputer

mands, rather than responding to typed commands. The Apple Macintosh operating system is the best known; other VOS include the Atari TOS, Digital Research Inc.'s "GEM" system, and the operating systems of work stations.

In addition, some manufacturers—notoriously, Apple and Commodore—use proprietary operating systems that are unique to their brand of PC. Small computers such as notebook and home computers do not have the memory or disk capacity for the standard operating systems, though the Japanese MSX operating system—which is designed for small computers—is found in a number of home computer systems sold outside the United States.

Operating an Operating System

Ninety percent of the work in any OS is done with 10% of the available functions. This section will discuss those functions and give examples of the commands for them in each of three OS—MS-DOS, UNIX, and the Apple Macintosh VOS. This is *not* a complete guide to those systems, but will provide a starting point and a sense of the most commonly used parts of the system. I am deliberately discussing the most common, rather than the most advanced, of these OS—all have upgrades more sophisticated than what I'm discussing.

The three systems discussed are very different and have completely different histories, so this section may appear to be comparing apples, oranges, and camels. To an extent that is true, but all three OS perform equivalent functions for the user. A brief discussion of each is in order before we begin.

MS-DOS was modeled after the original general purpose microcomputer OS, CP/M, and retains some of CP/M's structure and commands. CP/M, in turn, was modeled after mainframe OS. It is a "command-driven" OS, responding to typed commands from the user. I will focus on the early—and still most common—versions of MS-DOS, which had a *flat* file structure in which every file had to have a unique name.

UNIX was originally designed for mainframes, and it is based on a hard disk rather than a floppy disk. Like MS-DOS, it is command driven. UNIX uses a *hierarchical* file system that allows the disk to be organized into subdirectories; file names need be unique only within a subdirectory. UNIX's popularity among programmers and experienced computer users stems from the fact that it contains an extremely powerful set of programming and data manipulation tools that are beyond the scope of this introduction but that allow a knowledgeable user to handle very complex file transformations without writing special programs.

UNIX is notoriously unfriendly to the user, however, and requires considerable experience to use well. Many of the features of UNIX have been incorporated into advanced versions of other OS such as MS-DOS, and UNIX-like features are likely to become more common in PCs as hard disks become a standard feature of those computers.

Most UNIX commands are very short but mnemonic—for example, "cd" means "change directory." In the summaries I've provided an English interpretation of the command in brackets ([. . .]) after the command. Unlike some systems, only the proper command, not the English interpretation, will work: The commands are mnemonics, not abbreviations.

The OS of the Apple Macintosh is the first commercially successful VOS, and was based directly on the Xerox PARC work; it has all of the key characteristics of a VOS. It was controversial when first introduced—the mouse in particular is less than universally loved—but the VOS has proven to be much easier to learn than command-driven systems. The Macintosh commands take longer to describe in text because they are executed physically, with hand movements, rather than through text commands. The same commands that are awkward to describe are in fact quite fast and easy after a few minutes practice, and are more easily remembered than typed commands. As with MS-DOS, I will focus on the basic Macintosh system, which uses 3.5-inch floppy disks and a flat file system; newer versions of the Mac VOS have a hierarchical system.

1. Find the correct manuals. This is not as easy as it sounds, since manufacturers pride themselves on the amount of paper included with the PC. Make sure you've got the operating system manual and not the BASIC computer language manual or the installation/troubleshooting manual. If there is a "Beginner's Section" in the manual, work through it.

If you are totally new to a complex system such as UNIX or advanced versions of MS-DOS, it may be helpful to buy a book that provides a beginner's introduction. Such books are widely available at mass-market bookstores and are frequently excellent. There is no single best choice; browse until you find one at a level you are comfortable with.

2. Boot the system. This is easy—put the system disk in the boot disk drive, which is usually the left or top drive, and turn on the machine. Be sure you've got the OS disk that corresponds to the manual. UNIX boots automatically from the hard disk when the machine is turned on but then it may require a logging-in sequence just like a mainframe. Booting often takes a minute or so.

3. Learn the OS prompt character. There is usually a distinctive prompt character (e.g., "." "]" ">" "*") that indicates that the OS is waiting for commands. If the OS prompt appears while you are running a program, the program has probably crashed and passed control back to the OS.

VOS have no prompt character but instead present one or more "windows"; a cursor arrow moved by the mouse allows you to select items in the window.

4. Learn the disk drive names. In MS-DOS (and CP/M) the boot drive is called "A," the second floppy drive "B," and remaining drives C, D, E, and F. UNIX doesn't use drive names but instead works through subdirectories. Type the full directory name or use the "cd" (change directory) command to move into a subdirectory; use ".." to back out to the next highest directory. On the Mac, a little picture ("icon") of the disk appears on the right side of the screen and the disk has a name that is usually five to ten characters long.

5. Run a program. Locate a file that you know is a program (as opposed to data) and run it. See step 7 to list the directory. Frequently OS disks contain programs with some variation of the name DEMO that demonstrate the machine—try them. In MS-DOS executable programs have a suffix of .EXE or .COM.

MS-DOS, UNIX   Program file name.

| Macintosh | "Double-click" the file icon—place the cursor on the icon and press the mouse button twice quickly. |

6. Format a disk. Disks must be "formatted" or "initialized" before they can be used. During formatting the machine writes magnetic markers onto the disk that are subsequently used to locate information. Different computers format disks in different ways, so disks written by one type of PC often cannot be read by another.

Formatting *destroys any information on the disk*, so never format a disk unless you are sure it is blank or outdated. Many—but not all—systems will issue a warning before formatting an already-formatted disk. It is usually easier to format several disks at once—the process takes a couple of minutes and it is helpful to have formatted disks on hand. Also be sure that the disks are of the proper type for the machine you are using.

MS-DOS	FORMAT (program)
UNIX	Irrelevant to the hard disk; use "mkdir" (make directory) to create a new subdirectory.
Macintosh	Formatting program is invoked automatically for any unformatted or unreadable disk.

7. List the disk directory. The disk directory listing shows the files on the disk and usually information about the size and contents.

MS-DOS	DIR
UNIX	ls (lists the current subdirectory)
Macintosh	Double-click the disk icon.

8. List a text file to the screen. The contents of text files can be reviewed by listing them on the screen. While it is possible to "list" nontext files, this will rarely produce anything intelligible and may cause the screen to freeze, requiring a reboot or RESET to get the system functioning again.

MS-DOS	TYPE
UNIX	cat OR more
Macintosh	Double-click the file icon; this will cause the file automatically to invoke the program that created it and display the contents, provided that program is

available. Mac TEXT files can be opened through MacWrite and various desk accessories.

9. Stop the listing. With text scrolling by at 960 characters per second, you'll want to stop it, unless you read very fast. On many PCs, CTRL-S will do this; other machines have a PAUSE key. The IBM PC uses CTRL-NUMLOCK for this purpose. Most PCs use CTRL-Q to restart a listing, though some restart with another CTRL-S.

10. Print screen. Most systems have some means of automatically printing whatever is listed on the screen.

MS-DOS	CTRL-P
UNIX	lp (line printer)
Macintosh	Command-Caps Lock-Shift-4 key combination. The "command" key looks like a 4-leaf clover and is just to the left of the space bar.

11. Copy an entire disk. This is used to make backup copies.

MS-DOS	DISKCOPY program
UNIX	Not relevant; entire subdirectories can be copied using cp [copy] command.
Macintosh	Place the mouse cursor over the icon of the disk to be copied, hold the button down, and "drag" it onto the icon for the disk to be copied to.

Any disk that is frequently used, or expensive to replace, should be copied, the copy used, and the original stored safely. Data disks should be backed up frequently.

Some disks are "copy protected," so that they cannot be copied with standard routines. Some such disks can be copied with "bit copiers," which bypass the protection schemes; these are discussed in Chapter 7.

12. Learn the file name formats. Files have names that must follow a specific format. The usual format has the following form:

$$<\text{volume name}>: \quad <\text{file name}>$$

The volume name refers to the disk, or part of the disk, where the file resides. Referring to files by volume name avoids having to know the physical location of the file: The OS will search until it finds a disk with the correct volume name. The file name is given by the user, and is usually fairly short (8 to 10 characters). In most systems, files must start with a letter and cannot contain certain special characters (e.g., "?" "=" or "*"). Two files in a flat system or in a subdirectory cannot have exactly the same name.

MS-DOS file names have suffixes that identify the contents of the files. For example, if the file contains text, it has a suffix of .DAT; executable program code has the suffix .EXE or .COM; a Turbo Pascal program has a suffix .PAS.

UNIX uses "path names" to designate files; these would take about a chapter to explain fully—the reader is referred to a UNIX manual. The hierarchical versions of MS-DOS use a scheme very similar to that of UNIX.

The Macintosh user usually doesn't need to worry about file names because files are almost always selected from lists or via icons. The Macintosh distinguishes types of files by different shaped icons rather than suffixes, and various programs produce their own distinctive icons. File names can be up to 63 characters but in practice are kept much shorter.

13. Learn the "wildcard" formats. It is often useful to refer to a set of files rather than just a single file. "Wildcards" allow this to be done by telling the system to operate on all files with certain characters in their names, where the remaining characters can be anything. Wildcards considerably simplify the task of managing large numbers of related files.

As an example, files containing data from three days of research and a written summary might be named

TEST1.DAY1.DAT   TEST1.DAY2.DAT   TEST1.DAY3.DAT   TEST1.SUMM.TXT

Using the wildcard notation TEST1* in MS-DOS or UNIX, all four files can be manipulated using a single command.

Wildcard systems are confusing at first, so study the examples in the manual closely and experiment. The most common wildcard error is unintentionally matching a file. For example, the wildcards given above would match the file name TEST10.SUM.TXT, so an attempt to delete the TEST1 result would also delete TEST10. Matching with TEST1.* would solve the problem—the period after the 1 prevents matching on 10.SUM.TXT. Careful choice of file names and careful use of wildcards is very helpful when managing large sets of related files.

In the Macintosh, the equivalent of the wildcard is selecting a number of icons. This can be done by holding down the mouse button and moving the mouse to create a box around the relevant files, or holding down the shift button while selecting individual files. The selected group of files can then be manipulated as a group.

14. Delete or rename a file. As files are accumulated on a disk, periodic "housecleaning" is needed to delete old files. Occasionally it is also useful to rename files.

MS-DOS	Delete:	DEL
	Rename:	REN
UNIX	Delete:	rm (remove)
	Rename:	mv (move)
Macintosh	Delete:	Drag file icon into trash can at bottom of screen.
	Rename:	Click file to select, then type new name.

15. Copy individual files. Copying individual files is used to back up only a few files on a disk or rearrange the files in a set of disks.

MS-DOS	COPY
UNIX	cp (copy)
Macintosh	Click file to select, then type Command-D.

16. Compute free disk space. Disks hold a finite amount of information and it is useful to keep track of the available space. Free space and file sizes are usually reported in bytes and the total capacity of the disk depends on the hardware being used. In general, it is a very good idea not to let a disk get more than about 75% full—programs use disk space in unexpected and unpredictable ways to store information temporarily, and a disk 95% full may cause a program to fail. Know the disk capacity and keep track of how much is used.

MS-DOS	DIR
UNIX	available in the directory listing if appropriate options are selected; not usually an issue in a hard disk system
Macintosh	always displayed in upper-right corner of disk window

The capacity of a disk varies dramatically between programs and between computers. A 5-inch disk may hold anywhere from 140K bytes (Apple II) to over 1200K bytes. The size of a text file is usually slightly greater than the number of characters it contains. In numerical data, integers usually require two bytes per number; decimal numbers require four to eight bytes. Data-base programs and graphics systems differ substantially in their storage schemes and the practical disk capacity can be found only through experimentation.

17. Help. "Help" procedures are popular on mainframe operating systems and are found on more advanced microcomputer operating systems. A help procedure gives the syntax of a command and some indication of what it does. Help is usually invoked with the word HELP or the symbol "?." In UNIX, the "man" (manual) command will give help, albeit often with pages from the UNIX manual, a document known for specificity rather than clarity. On the Mac, help is usually found under the small apple character in the upper-left corner of the window.

18. Security systems. Most operating systems provide a limited form of file security, particularly against files being accidentally erased or overwritten. MS-DOS and UNIX allow a file to be designated "read-only" (R/O), which means the file can be read but not overwritten or deleted. Both systems also allow files to be encrypted with password systems. The Macintosh provides a lock option in the files information block that prevents files from being changed without being unlocked first; utility programs can be used to make a file "invisible" so that it does not appear on a regular directory listing (though it will be listed for a utility program).

19. Learn to restart the system. Systems will sooner or later "hang up," "crash," "freeze," "bomb," or otherwise cease operating correctly when you do something that the system particularly dislikes. In such instances it is usually possible to "warm boot" the system and restart it. A warm boot is slightly faster than turning the machine off and on, and less stressful for the machine. The IBM PC uses the three-key combination CTRL-ALT-DEL for a warm boot; the Macintosh should have a button on the back left side of the machine, though sometimes it isn't installed.

If the memory occupied by the OS has been overwritten, warm booting and RESET may not work, in which case you must turn the machine off and boot it again. If this happens frequently, the machine is probably overheating—let it cool, and check to be sure the ventilation holes aren't blocked.

Advanced: File Manipulation

In an ideal world, any program could read files created by any other program, and consequently exchanging information between programs would be a simple matter of writing and reading disk files. Unfortunately, the situation is not so simple.

In general, files that are not alphanumeric text can be read only by the program that created them. This is often the case for data-base, statistics, and graphics programs. Programs *designed* to be used together can share files, but this is the exception rather than the rule, so do not assume that two programs will be able to read the same files. Data storage formats used by popular programs have become de facto standards for files in related programs. For example, a number of CP/M and MS-DOS programs can use the DIF (Data Interchange Format), which originated with VisiCorp's VisiCalc program.

Alphanumeric text files are usually stored in the standard ASCII code (American Standard Code for Information Interchange). Consequently, programs running under the same OS can often share text files even if they cannot share other files. Text can be transferred between different makes of computer by connecting the two machines via modems, or by transferring text to a third computer (uploading) and then having the recipient machine read the text from that computer (downloading) (see Chapter 9).

Information about the files is stored in the *disk directory*. The directory contains the names of the files, their size, location on the disk, and frequently other information such as the creation date and type. The directory is also the most vulnerable part of the disk, and damage to the directory may prevent the OS from reading any of the files on the disk. In such cases a patch program must be used to recover the files (see Chapter 2).

Patch programs can also frequently be used to recover a file that has been inadvertently deleted, provided the file itself has not been overwritten. Utility programs such as the Norton Utilities for MS-DOS machines and MacTools for the Macintosh will do this reconstruction automatically. You will usually end up with a lot of junk files that need to be discarded and some recent work may be lost, but it beats rebuilding an entire disk.

Files are stored on a disk with some error checking, and if a disk has deteriorated attempting to read it will result in a message such as BDOS ERR or DISK READ ERROR. This means the error checking indicates the disk is being read incorrectly, and so the OS refuses to process it. If a disk has been only slightly damaged most of the information will still be intact, but the error checking in the OS must be bypassed using a patch program. It is also possible to damage a disk beyond repair, either physically or electronically. Code and data files are more vulnerable to damage than text files, since even a single incorrect bit may cause problems when the file is used.

Troubleshooting

Since the operating system is the fundamental control program for the PC, major errors usually require shutting off the machine (or using

RESET) and starting over. Nonetheless, here are a few common errors:

Operating system won't boot. First, be sure the disk is in the correct drive, and correctly inserted. Second, be sure the monitor is turned on—the disk may have booted but is not being displayed. Third, be sure you actually have a boot disk. Finally, try the disk in another machine; if it doesn't boot there, it is probably damaged—make another copy and try again. *Don't* use the original copy of the disk to check the machine— the drive may be damaging disks, even if they are write-protected.

Disk read error. Again, several possibilities. First, be sure the disk is formatted for the machine it is being used on. Second, the disk may have been damaged by any of the various means mentioned in Chapter 2. Third, the timing on the drive may be off—try the disk in another drive. Fourth, the disk may be copy-protected so that it cannot be read. Finally, the drive may be acting erratically due to heat or electrical supply—try reading the disk a couple of times before giving up on it.

Disk full. Generally, this means the disk cannot hold any more information—delete some files. In some situations, the OS may think a disk is full when it isn't, because the system has reserved all of the remaining space on the disk. These situations simply have to be avoided through experience and are mentioned only to indicate that it is possible to get a DISK FULL error on what appears to be an empty disk.

System ceases to respond. First, check to be sure you haven't pressed CTRL-S or some other key sequence that stops the machine. If that doesn't work, some program has probably overwritten the OS and you'll need to reboot. The RESET keys may have been disabled in the process, so turning the machine off and on may be necessary.

Disk drives whir incessantly. The operating system may be looking for an important program (e.g., itself) that it can't find—be sure the correct disk is in the drive. On a few older machines, continual operation of the disk is normal.

4. EDITORS AND WORD PROCESSING

The computer started life as a numerical processor, and grew up doing physics, accounting, and processing income tax returns. While microcomputers are quite capable of numerical processing, their most common use is probably word processing. The descendants of the electronic behemoths designed to compute ballistic trajectories and atomic collisions now spend the bulk of their time moving letters around.

If you have never used a word processor, you are in for both joy and a bit of frustration. A text editor removes the concept of a "draft." A manuscript does not proceed from first to second to final draft; instead it grows organically, and pieces are added and deleted at will. Unfortunately, machines also occasionally delete things you'd prefer to save, leaving a blank screen and two hours of wasted effort, and that is where the frustration comes.

Text editing is not limited to manuscripts. Program input such as data, graphics commands, program source code, and data base management routines are all possible products of a text editor. Word processing systems differ tremendously in their capabilities, but all revolve around a few very simple functions. This chapter will discuss how to learn to use a word processor; the details of any specific system can be learned from the system manual.

Introduction: Editors and Formatters

A word processing system consists of three parts: an *editor*, a *formatter*, and some form of *file management*. The editor inserts, deletes, and changes text in a file. A formatter takes that text, modifies the file to include various printing directives (spacing, typeface, and so forth) and transmits it to the printer. The file management system handles disk directories, deletion of files, and so forth, and may or may not be similar to the operating system of the computer. In the more integrated word processors, the editor, formatter, and file management are combined in a single program; in less integrated systems, the functions are separate.

In general there are two different types of editors: *line* editors and *screen* editors. In a line editor, each line of text has a number, and changes are made by referring to a particular line or set of lines. A screen editor, in contrast, works with the text as it appears on the CRT, without line numbers. Text is changed by moving a cursor to the point where characters are to be inserted or deleted, and making the change on the screen. Screen editors are far easier to use than line editors, and most PCs use them.

Formatters also come in two types, "embedded command" (EC) and "what you see is what you get" (WYSIWYG) formatters. EC formatters use special control codes to indicate paragraphs, centering, and other printing controls. The text file is rearranged to specifications by the formatter, so the original file can be very sloppy. In WYSIWYG formatters the display of the page on the screen looks exactly as it will appear on the printed page. Most newer word processors are

WYSIWYG, except those specifically designed for setting tables or some types of scientific notation.

The advantage of the WYSIWYG formatter is complete control over the appearance of the final document without having to second-guess the formatter. The only drawback is that very little formatting is automated. EC formatters are very forgiving of input, and some contain sophisticated facilities for automatic arrangement of tables, equations, and other standard material. However, a document formatted with embedded commands must usually be printed a couple of times to get everything working correctly, and the system takes longer to learn as a consequence.

"Program formatters" are available for rearranging the text of computer programs for easy reading. These are useful in structured programming languages such as Pascal and C. The formatters recognize key words that delineate related blocks of program code and indent the text accordingly. The program formatters can also do elementary syntax checking—for example, balancing parentheses.

The file management in a word processing system is usually similar to the machine's operating system. Most systems use standard ASCII files, which allow the editor to prepare input for programs and modify files downloaded from other systems.

Operation: Editing

Editors appear complicated, yet most editing requires only a very limited set of operations. By learning these first, and worrying about the complications later, an editor can be learned in a few minutes. On one occasion I was using an unfamiliar mainframe over a long-distance phone line and needed to leave a message, and figured out the system's editor by trial-and-error in a couple of minutes: Editors are not very complicated.

To get started, find the manuals and get the editor running. Word processing manuals, unlike operating system manuals, tend to be friendly and almost always have a Beginner's Section that takes you through the basic steps. Follow this through, but keep in mind that there are only six things you need to know at first.

1. Save and retrieve a file. Try to create a file, save it, and get it back again before doing anything else. Don't wait until you've written something worth saving before doing this. Experiment with file management: List the disk directory and determine whether the disk is getting full.

All editors are limited in the amount of text held in memory at a given time. Some automatically "swap" text to and from the disk as needed, so file length is not a problem. On less sophisticated systems, a long document must be divided into a number of files, usually five to ten pages each, which are then "chained" together for printing. It is a good idea not to allow a single file to get too close to the limit, since this may impede other features of the program, notably the copy-and-move feature.

2. Cursor movements. If you are using a screen editor, learn how to move the cursor sideways, up, and down. Cursor movements should be governed by the cursor keys, though some older programs use CTRL commands. In a line editor, learn how to change the line number. Most programs will move the cursor a full page up or down, and move to the beginning or end of the file. In many programs "markers" can be placed in a file and the cursor directed to them. Rapid cursor movement is important in the efficient use of an editor.

3. Insert and delete. These are the two most frequent operations. When inserting, most programs have an auto-return feature, which automatically returns the cursor to the next line when the end of a line is reached. When deleting, check for features that allow large amounts of text to be deleted—for example, many editors have a "Delete to end of line" command and can delete entire words or lines with a single keystroke.

4. Replace. Replace commands combine a delete and an insert. Most screen editors have two types of replace. One option exchanges: New text is typed over old. This is efficient if the two sets of text are the same length.

Alternatively, a "target string" can be specified and replaced with a substitute. A string is just a set of characters delimited with a special character (for instance, / or "). The string can be matched to any occurrence or just to isolated words. Thus it is possible to specify whether the substitution of the string /micro/ for the target /computer/ would operate on *any* occurrence of the target—for example changing "microcomputer" to "micromicro"—or just on the word "computer" occurring alone.

Usually a replace substitutes only for the first occurrence of the target after the cursor. A "global replace" modifies all of the occurrences of the target in a file. Global replaces can have unexpected effects, so be careful. It may also be possible to ask for verification before replacing.

Targeted replace commands appear at first to be more complicated than exchanges, but for a good typist they are faster. Even though two strings must be specified in a targeted replace, the time spent in cursor movement and matching string length is greater in the exchange replace.

5. Copy and move. Editors can move text from one part of a file to another place in the file. This is the electronic equivalent of cutting out some text and pasting it elsewhere.

Copying is done using one of two techniques. One approach uses markers—either special characters, line numbers, or invisible pointers—at the beginning and end of the text to be moved. The cursor is moved (or line number changed) to the new location, and the "move" or "copy" command transfers the delineated text.

An alternative approach stores deleted text in a buffer, which can hold a large number of characters. Text is transferred by deleting it (which transfers the text to the buffer) then copying the text from the buffer at the new location. To copy without destroying the original text, the buffer is first recopied at the original location, then again at the new location. When using this method be careful not to lose the buffer contents; for example, deciding to delete more text before first copying existing text will usually clear the buffer.

6. Merging files. Text can be moved from one file into another file. This is frequently necessary when maximum file size is limited. Merging is usually done by moving the cursor (or line number) to the point where the new material will be inserted, then the merge command requests the name of the file containing the new material.

When merging files, be sure that the combined files are not too long for the editor. For this reason, it is also a good idea to keep files well below the maximum size allowed by the program—75% of maximum is a good figure—so that most inserts and merges can be done without having to split the file in half. If a file needs to be split, save the original file, then delete half, save the remaining half under a new name, retrieve the original, delete the other half, and then save the remainder.

That's it for the basics! These six operations will account for most of the work in an editor, and can be learned in a short time. Learn them, practice with them, and only then try any advanced features of the editor.

Operation: Formatting

Formatting is dependent on the capabilities of the printer and the word processing system, but a number of functions are common to all formatters. On WYSIWYG systems many of these functions are done in the editor, but some may require embedded commands. In EC systems most formatting is done with embedded commands.

1. Page and spacing control. It should be possible to switch between single and double spacing, and to force a page eject before the end of a page. Fine control of vertical spacing, e.g., 1/72 inch (0.3 mm), may also be possible.

2. Margin control and right-justification. All programs provide some means of setting margins. In WYSIWYG programs, this is done on the screen. EC programs adjust margins as they format the text. It should also be possible to turn off the margin adjustment facility for tables, indented material, and figures. Many printers will, if requested, automatically right-justify text (i.e., make the right margin even, as in most typeset material) and some formatters will do this.

3. Page numbering and headings. All formatters number pages, and most allow the page number to be placed at one of several places on the page. Page headings and footings can also be specified. Many systems allow alternative heading and number placement depending on whether the page number is even or odd, which allows booklike typesetting.

4. Footnotes. Some word processing programs designed for the academic community can manage the placement and numbering of footnotes automatically, but this is not a feature in all programs. If footnotes are an important consideration, check this feature carefully.

5. Alternative typefaces. Most printers provide at least boldface, and many dot-matrix printers provide italics. These are usually controlled with embedded commands. On some printers it is possible to switch to entirely different character fonts, such as katakana, Cyrillic, or Greek. A variety of programs can produce elaborate typefaces like those used in headlines and posters (e.g., Old English) on dot matrix printers, and some have been integrated into formatters.

6. Centering and tab stops. On WYSIWYG programs, these are done on the screen; in EC programs tab and centering controls are embedded in the text. These controls can save tremendous amounts of time when dealing with tables, outlines, and other tabular text.

7. Superscripts and subscripts. These require that the printer be able to perform a vertical "backspace" or else print special superscript and subscript characters. These are usually specified with embedded commands.

8. Special control sequences. The special functions of any printer can be controlled by sending the proper sequence of ASCII characters, usually prefixed by the ESC character (ASCII 27). Most programs allow an arbitrary control sequence to be sent to the printer using embedded controls. This would allow, for example, the superscript facility of the printer to be used even if the formatter didn't specifically provide for superscripts.

9. Chain files. If an editor limits the maximum size of a file, the formatter will chain files together so that several files can be printed as a single document. In most systems chaining is set at the time the files are printed, though in some systems an embedded command at the end of a file specifies the next file in the chain.

Advanced: Word Processing

Word processing programs are probably the most elaborate software currently available for PCs in terms of possible options. This section will briefly mention some supplemental features that are available, usually at an additional cost. Currently no PC program contains all of these, and acquiring all would involve a substantial outlay of money (perhaps $1000-$1500), but they are available.

1. Spelling. These programs go through a text file and check each word against a dictionary. Any words that are not in that dictionary are then marked as possibly misspelled. The programs are relatively slow and to operate well require both a large dictionary and the ability to add words to that dictionary. A related program is the electronic *Thesaurus*, which provides a display of synonyms for designated words.

2. Automatic index and bibliography preparation. Some programs will automatically tabulate and format an index, bibliography, and table of contents. This information is delineated within the text file itself (e.g., the bibliographic information can be placed anywhere in the text) and then tabulated by the formatter.

3. Mailing list and form letters. Mailing lists can be created and updated using the editor, then mailing list information can be incorporated into the body of a letter. The technique is by now familiar to everyone; the programs are relatively simple to use.

4. Style checking. Programs have been developed for word processing computers and minicomputers that check "style" by looking for average word, sentence, and paragraph length, cliché phrases, and so forth.

5. Outline processor. This is essentially an electronic outline that can be easily expanded and contracted. It allows one to write a manuscript by starting with an outline and then gradually filling in the outline with text. The manuscript can be printed at any stage in either text or outline form. The "Think Tank" program was the first and is still the most popular program of this genre.

6. Desktop publishing. These programs are most commonly found on the Macintosh and other VOS machines with high-resolution graphics screens. They are designed for the production of typeset-quality documents, usually on a laser printer, and include facilities for handling columnar typesetting, half-tone photographs, highlighting and shading, color overlays, and other graphic techniques.

7. *Graphics and equations.* With dot matrix printers, graphics material can be printed as easily as text, though to date only a few systems can combine text and graphics. A very successful system for typesetting equations, "eqn," has been developed for the UNIX system; Donald Knuth's general-purpose typesetting program TEX (pronounced "tech") is now available for a number of PC/printer combinations.

8. *Integration.* It should be possible to take information out of any program—for example, a data base—and insert it into a printed document. While this type of program integration is more common now than it was five years ago—and integration on the Macintosh is particularly well done—it still cannot be assumed. If it would be helpful to be able to transfer information frequently between, say, a data base or statistical program and a word processor, be sure that the two are compatible.

At the present time a major limitation of word processing programs is that they cannot use files from other word processors, except under very unusual circumstances. This includes files from different word processing programs on the same computer, as well as disks from different computers. Frequently the only way to transfer material is with a communications program (see Chapter 9).

Troubleshooting: Printers

The linkage between word processing systems and printers is one of the most complex and least standardized facets of microcomputing. Most programs need to be configured for a specific printer, and if this is not done correctly, parts of the program will not work. There is little that can be generally said about this configuration, and it is best left to someone who has studied the printer and the program thoroughly. The interface is not simple.

Dot-matrix and impact printers do not replace a duplicating machine. Even fast printers are fairly slow, and they are in some danger of overheating if they run for long periods of time. The economies of scale favor the photocopying machine for more than two or three copies. While 120 characters per second sounds fast, it translates to a half-minute per page, so a twenty-page document takes ten minutes to print. Truly high-speed printers require more expensive technology—chain, ink-jet, electrostatic, and laser printing—than is presently available for most PCs.

Most word processors allow previewing a formatted file on the screen before it is printed. This is useful since formatting is almost never correct the first time, particularly if the editor doesn't show page breaks. Previewing output on the screen saves time and paper and isolates the formatting problems from the printer problems.

Before trying to print a document, be sure that the printer is plugged in, turned on, has paper correctly loaded, and has a clear path for the paper into the machine and somewhere for the paper to pile up after it leaves the machine. Adjust the paper so that the top of the sheet is aligned with the printing head, and if the printer has a SET TOF (top-of-form) switch, press it. Then hope.

PROBLEM: Printer does nothing.

SOLUTION: Is the printer plugged in and turned on? Is it connected to the computer? Is it ready to print? Ejecting paper often requires a switch to be turned off to prevent the machine from printing, and this may have been left off by the previous user. Does the printer have paper and is the paper fed correctly? Check the paper feed carefully; the printer may seem to have paper and still not think it has paper if the paper is incorrectly routed.

PROBLEM: Computer prints garbage on a file that was previously okay.

SOLUTION: Printers have switches that set various printer modes. These are usually on the front panel, possibly hidden so that you won't notice and change them. The previous user may have reset these to print boldface, 132-characters across, for instance. Determine the correct settings (this will vary between printers), then reinitialize the printer by switching it off and on. Simply changing the switches may not work, since many printers read the switches only when they are first turned on. *Total* garbage can occur when there is a magnetic field interfering with the cable from the computer to the printer, for example an electric cord or tape recorder. Check for a clear path between the two.

PROBLEM: Printer stops after each page.

SOLUTION: It is waiting for another single sheet of paper. If you are using continuous paper, turn off this feature.

PROBLEM: Printer stops in the middle of a page.

SOLUTION: Several possible problems. First, the paper may be about to run out; check this first. Check whether the ribbon has jammed or (on carbon ribbons) run out. The printer may be waiting for a change in type wheels (intentionally or otherwise), an accidental CTRL character may have stopped it, or the operating system may have been unable to find a file.

PROBLEM: Paper doesn't move, so that lines are printed on top of each other.

SOLUTION: Automatic linefeed is OFF when it should be ON. Reset switches and reinitialize printer.

PROBLEM: Printer double spaces when it should be single spacing and quadruple spaces when it should double space.

SOLUTION: Automatic linefeed is ON when it should be OFF. Reset switches and reinitialize printer.

PROBLEM: Printer begins printing garbage in the middle of a line, then corrects itself on next line.

SOLUTION: There is probably an incorrect control character embedded in the text line, which may have been placed there when you accidently hit the ALT or CTRL key. Remove it.

PROBLEM: Printer begins to continuously underline, boldface, subscript, or some other feature.

SOLUTION: You probably forgot to turn off the feature in question. Alternatively, a line may contain control characters. Retype the offending line.

PROBLEM: Formatted pages longer or shorter than physical pages.

SOLUTION: The formatter or the printer thinks that you are using a different paper size than you are using. Check printer switches first, then check formatting commands.

PROBLEM: Page ejects in illogical places or a totally blank page.

SOLUTION: Override the formatter with forced page ejects. The formatter may not share your esthetic values. Blank pages result when a forced page eject coincides with the formatted end of page, so the formatter ejects one page on its own, then a second on command.

PROBLEM: Printing is very faint.

SOLUTION: Probably the ribbon is worn out; replace it. Also check the pressure adjustment: pressure may have been adjusted such that the pressure on a single sheet is too light.

PROBLEM: Printing is sporadically faint.

SOLUTION: Ribbon is occasionally jamming, or has worn sections due to earlier jams. Replace with a new ribbon. A good ribbon is needed for quality printing, and printers in social science computer labs tend to have worn ribbons: Buy your own.

5. PROGRAMMING

The computer is unique in its almost infinite flexibility to be *programmed* to do different tasks. A typewriter is a typewriter, an adding machine is an adding machine, an index file is an index file, but with suitable programs a computer can be all three, and much more. The concept of a stored program is the single most revolutionary aspect of the computer.

In the early days of computing, programming was portrayed as a complex and esoteric art, reserved for physics Ph.D.s and presided over by a technocratic elite with restricted access to The Machine. Nowadays programming is taught in grade schools, a more appropriate level. Elementary programming is not trivial, but it is no more difficult, and considerably more enjoyable, than long division or high school geometry. Furthermore, microcomputers have made programming more interesting through sound and graphics. Whereas the typical first assignment in a mainframe programming class was computation of prime numbers or sales totals, the first assignment on a PC is likely to be the creation of a computer piano, the drawing of spirals, or the programming of an animated ball bouncing around the screen.

It is possible to use a PC without knowing any programming, but to exploit fully the capabilities of the machine, programming is helpful. Writing a few programs aids in comprehending how software works and helps avoid mistakes when using programs.

Introduction: What Is a Program?

A computer—any computer—can essentially do only four things:

- read and write memory,
- read and write to external devices (input/output),
- do arithmetic operations on numbers, and
- compare two numbers to see which is larger and do different things depending on the result

All other functions of the computer are built out of these very simple operations.

As an illustration of programming, suppose you have left your house plants in the care of a friend who knows nothing about house plants. The friend demands step-by-step instructions, and so you prepare a list of numbered index cards:

1. Get the watering can.

2. Get a blank piece of paper and a pencil.

3. Go to the kitchen.

4. Turn on the water faucet.

5. Put water in the can.

6. Go to the living room.

7. Find a plant.

8. Check if the plant has been watered. If Yes, go to card 12.

9. Water the plant.

10. Is there still water in the watering can? If No, go to cards 100-104.

11. Make a mark on the paper.

12. Are there 12 marks on the paper? If No, go to card 7.

13. Go to the dining room

   (etc.).

   . . . .

100. (* subroutine for filling water can *)

101. Go to the kitchen.

102. Turn on the faucet.

103. Fill the water can.

104. Go to card after subroutine call.

Now, leaving aside the fact that this "program" would be appropriate only for a very stupid—but literate—friend (an apt description of a computer), consider how it works. The program is "initialized" in the first five cards, which ensure that the friend has paper, a full watering can, and is in the living room before doing anything else. Subsequent cards are followed in numerical order, except when that order is changed by "conditional statements" such as 8, 10, and 12. Statements 7 to 12 are an example of a "loop," which tells the friend to keep watering plants until all 12 plants in the living room have been watered. The program continues in this loop until all plants are watered, at which point it branches to another part of the program—card 13, the dining room. A "subroutine" is a section of code that is used in more than one place in the program; for example notice that cards 3, 4, and 5 could be replaced by the single statement "GOTO subroutine 100."

Detailed as this program is, it still contains "bugs"—unintended results that would cause problems. For example, to prevent flooding, the subroutine should probably have an additional card:

103.5 Turn off the faucet.

The current version leaves the friend in the kitchen: it should instruct the friend to return to the room he or she was in before the subroutine call. The program also needs some error checking. For example, if there were only eleven plants in the room, the friend would never leave the living room loop; this is called an infinite loop. It could be changed by an error check such as, "Are there 12 plants in the room? If No, call the exterminator, darn cockroaches again . . ." Anticipating all possible bugs and errors is difficult; finding and correcting them is called debugging.

Computer programs are written at roughly the same level of detail as shown in this example, except that they deal with the manipulation of numbers and letters rather than friends and house plants. A general scheme for performing a task on a computer is called an algorithm; a program is a specific implementation of an algorithm.

Programs are written in programming languages, which use words and symbols resembling natural or mathematical language. The microprocessor itself understands only "machine language," which consists solely of numbers. The earliest computers were painstakingly programmed using numbers, but quickly it was realized that the computer could be used to translate worded instructions into the numerical machine language, and so high-level languages evolved. Several hundred programming languages exist, though only a dozen or so are in common use.

Programming languages are usually either "interpreted" or "compiled." In an interpreted language, an interpreter takes each statement as it is encountered, translates it into machine language, then feeds the machine language to the CPU, which executes it. Interpreters require little memory and are simple to run, but are slow because statements must be repeatedly translated. A compiler, on the other hand, goes through the entire program and translates it into machine code before the program is run. Compilers require longer to prepare a program to run, but the resulting code is faster. In addition to translating statements, both interpreters and compilers must do extensive work managing memory, and some compilers attempt to optimize for speed while translating.

There are several different programming languages because trade-offs exist within each language, and different languages are designed for different purposes. In addition to general purpose languages such as BASIC and Pascal, there are special-purpose languages for fields such as artificial intelligence, simulation, mathematics, and business programming. While any operations on any data can be done by any language, the real question is how *efficiently* the task is done in terms of programming time and program speed. Certain tasks difficult in one language may be simple in another.

Operation: BASIC, Pascal, and Assembler

At the present time, three languages dominate the programming of microcomputers: BASIC, Pascal, and assembly language. They evolved separately and, thus, have distinct disadvantages and advantages.

Language	Main advantages	Main disadvantages

BASIC	easy to learn
	requires little
	  software support
		slow
		nonstandard
		encourages
		  messy code

Pascal	fast execution
	encourages
	  clean code
	standard
		requires major
		  software support
		  and memory
		inflexible

Assembly	very fast
	can utilize
	  all machine
	  capabilities
		machine dependent
		tedious to code

BASIC

BASIC was developed by John Kemeny at Dartmouth University in the 1960s as a simplified language for teaching computer programming. The language was originally used on mainframe computers with remote terminals, and originally included matrix operations that have since dropped out of the language. In large part, BASIC is derived from the dominant academic computing language of the time, FORTRAN.

BASIC was the first higher-level language implemented for micro-computers, having the joint advantages of being easy to learn and requiring little memory. Some form of BASIC is available on all PCs, and MicroSoft's M-BASIC dialect is available for most. MicroSoft, having been responsible for the first PC BASIC interpreter, has set what might be loosely called a standard for the language on microcomputers. BASIC has a logical structure similar to the dominant 1960s languages—academic FORTRAN and business COBOL. A massive software base exists in BASIC, and it is the most widely published language for micros.

Despite its popularity, BASIC has several disadvantages. First, it is usually interpreted and, hence, slow; a statement inside a loop has to be retranslated many, many times. Second, BASIC is not very sophisticated in terms of program structure, input/output, or data structures. This makes the language easy to learn but awkward in advanced applications. Third, the lack of standardization means that BASIC programs frequently must be virtually rewritten to be transferred to new machines. The slow speed of interpreted BASIC can be largely alleviated by BASIC compilers, which convert the BASIC code to machine language, which does not need to be interpreted.

A number of modified versions of BASIC have been developed to get around the language's drawbacks. These add features and impose additional constraints, and generally give BASIC better hardware control and better structure. Unfortunately, the hybrids further complicate the standardization problem, since they diverge to an extent that converting between some dialects is not only difficult but practically impossible without writing assembly language routines to replace the missing features for hardware control, data structures, and file controls.

BASIC is an excellent first language. The BASICs of most computers allow easy access to hardware capabilities such as graphics, game paddles, and sound generation, and adding assembly language routines to BASIC programs is usually simple. Speed can be increased with BASIC compilers in place of interpreters, and the outdated logical structure can be bypassed with good programming discipline. On the other hand, BASIC is based on programming languages from the 1950s and, thus, does not really lead anywhere, which is a substantial problem if one wishes to learn serious programming. Most advanced programming languages are very much unlike BASIC.

PASCAL

Pascal was designed by Niklaus Wirth at ETH Zurich and, like

BASIC, was also originally intended as a teaching language and has evolved into a general-purpose language. Pascal is based on the 1960s international standard programming language ALGOL, and shares most of ALGOL's keywords and program structures. It adds to ALGOL a far richer set of data structures, and a slightly easier syntax.

The wide acceptance of Pascal on microcomputers is due in part to the development, under Kenneth Bowles at the University of California, San Diego, of the UCSD p-System. The p-System was an entire operating system designed around an extended version of Wirth's Pascal, and included a sophisticated text editor and file management system. The p-System became a model for other PC Pascals, notably Phillipe Kahn's fabulously successful Turbo Pascal for the IBM PC and Apple Macintosh. Turbo Pascal is now the de facto standard for Pascal on PCs, even though it differs in several significant respects from the International Standards Organization (ISO) *official* standard Pascal.

Pascal generally takes longer to learn than BASIC, both because the p-System is complicated, and the language itself is more complex. Pascal employs a programming technique called structured programming (see below) and is compiled rather than interpreted. The payoff is that large Pascal programs are easier to debug and maintain than BASIC programs of comparable complexity. The structure of Pascal is closer to that of advanced languages such as Ada, C, and Modula-2; hence, it provides a good starting point for learning new languages.

Pascal is not without flaws. It makes more demands on system resources than BASIC, and usually must be compiled, introducing another step into the debugging process. Most Pascals are not intended to operate with individual words of machine memory, though they usually can do so via some well-known programming tricks. The language is not fully standardized: Wirth's original did not provide good facilities for text or graphics and adding these facilities has caused inconsistencies among implementations of the language.

ASSEMBLY LANGUAGE

Assembly language uses the instruction set of the microprocessor itself, with only a minimum of translation. Assembly language gives full and complete control of the machine, with no restrictions, but is tedious to write compared to higher-level languages.

Assembly language is not identical to machine language but very close to it. While machine language can be used directly by the CPU, assembly language must first be passed through an assembler, which does some simple translation. Assemblers, unlike interpreters and compilers, make very little modification of the code, and the major advantage of assembly language over machine language is that it is more readable. Assembly requires considerably more statements than high-level languages. For example,

| BASIC | 10 | C = A + B |
| Pascal | | C := A + B; |

			[Comment]
Assembler	LDA	A	Load accumulator with A
	ADC	B	Add value of B
	STA	C	Store result in C

The assembly language program requires three lines of instructions for the single line of BASIC or Pascal. While this is a trivial issue in a simple adding instruction, it becomes problematic in longer programs. Assembly language programs are also relatively difficult to read, unless they have been well documented, and their structure is virtually unpredictable.

Assembly language programming requires far more attention to the actual structure of the microprocessor and the PC itself than does programming in higher languages. Assembly language programs cannot be transferred between different microprocessors without being rewritten. Assembly language generally requires attention to machine architecture as well as algorithms, since the structure of different micro-processors can vary substantially.

Assembly language is *fast*. Short assembly language routines operate in a few thousandths of a second. The smooth animation of a well-written PC video game is impossible in BASIC or even in compiled Pascal. Assembly language is also necessary to customize input/output interfaces or otherwise modify the internal functions of the machine. If something can be done within the capabilities of the machine, it is possible to do it in assembly language.

There are dozens of introductory books covering each of these three programming languages, and it is possible to find books specifically designed for the more widely selling PCs. While in the past most people learned programming by taking a class, it is probably just as easy to do so by working through an introductory book. The emphasis here is *working through*. Learning programming is like learning a musical instrument: Practice is mandatory and reading alone doesn't go very far. Most people find programming at least mildly enjoyable, and the skills acquired by learning to program games are easily transferred to other work.

Advanced: Other Programming Languages

While for many people a single programming language is sufficient, it is often useful to know more than one. Specialized languages can simplify programming in some areas, and often learning a second language improves programming in the first. Once two or three programming languages are mastered, additional languages are relatively simple.

This section will briefly introduce some additional programming languages. *Some* implementation of each of these languages exists for some PCs, though in the case of the more complex languages (COBOL, Ada, LISP) it may be a partial implementation. Most compilers and interpreters cost between $200 and $500.

FORTRAN

Developed in the mid-1950s by John Backus of IBM, FORTRAN (FORmula TRANslation) became the standard progamming language for science and engineering, and is a precursor to BASIC. It is a compiled language and is widely available on micros.

There is a massive base of mainframe software available in FORTRAN, but it will probably be replaced by Pascal eventually. Anything FORTRAN can do Pascal can do just as easily, and Pascal can do it more with data structures. FORTRAN is unstructured and handles text poorly. Mainframe FORTRAN compilers have been perfected over three decades, though some PC implementations are very inefficient.

COBOL

This was the first standardized language and is the most common language for mainframe business applications. It is verbose but has excellent file manipulation capabilities. A variety of PC implementations of COBOL are available. However, the design of the language is thoroughly outdated and the only reason to use COBOL is to take advantage of some previously written program to manipulate large amounts of previously entered data.

C, FORTH, AND LOGO

C is a popular language for systems design, and is fast becoming one of the most popular languages for professional programmers. The language combines the structure and standardization of Pascal with an instruction set close to assembly language and, consequently, can be used to write fast code that is readable and easily moved to new machines. C is closely associated with the UNIX operating system and works best in a UNIX environment, though C compilers are available for most systems. It is relatively easy to learn if you know Pascal and some assembly.

FORTH and LOGO are related in structure to C and are popular in some applications. FORTH was used as a systems development language on some early PCs in part because the interpreters occupied very little memory. LOGO is designed as a teaching language for children and makes extensive use of graphics.

LISP AND PROLOG

LISP is the most common language used in artificial intelligence (AI) research and is particularly powerful as a tool for symbol manipulation. LISP has an unusual syntax relying heavily on functions and recursion, and for a while had diverged into a variety of incompatible dialects. In recent years there has been a movement toward establishing a standard "Common LISP" to provide compatibility, and this effort appears to be succeeding. A variety of PC implementations of LISP (in various dialects) are available.

Prolog is an AI-oriented language designed for programming rule-based expert systems. Like LISP, there are a number of incompatible dialects and, unlike LISP, there is substantial disagreement as to what a "standard" Prolog would look like. Various PC implementations are available, including several in the public domain.

APL

APL is a very powerful language for mathematical work, particularly when matrix algebra is involved. It employs an extraordinarily diverse character set and is next to impossible to read, but (and because) it can define complex sets of mathematical operations more compactly than any other programming language. APL is usually interpreted rather than compiled, and thus enables a PC to be used as a matrix "calculator."

ADA

The Department of Defense is attempting to standardize all of its software by converting to a single language, Ada. Ada is structured, compiled, and very complex; in spirit it is the 1980s descendent of the 1970s super-language PL/I. It is unclear at the moment whether *any* working Ada compilers exist—the language is so complex that compiler validation is difficult—and only subsets are available on PCs. Ada has yet to attract an enthusiastic following, though the Department of Defense imprimatur will guarantee survival in the near term.

MODULA-2

This is Nicklaus Wirth's modification of Pascal, which adds elements for text processing, input/output, and hardware control missing in Pascal, and makes the structure even more modular than Pascal's. Only a limited number of compilers are available at the moment, but in the long run Modula-2 may replace Pascal in professional programming.

Advanced: Programming Techniques

Most of the suggestions given below come from the literature and experience of professional programmers accustomed to writing large programs that have to be maintained over time by many people. At first glance, they have little applicability to the average programmer writing a short routine for him- or herself. However, after programming a while, you will be ready to start paying attention to some of these suggestions.

1. Use structured programming. During the late 1960s it became apparent that computer programs were becoming too complex to maintain or even verify, and that the existing programming practices found in COBOL and FORTRAN were a source of these problems. Structured programming, first advocated by Dutch mathematician Edsger Dijkstra and incorporated into most post-1970 languages (notably Pascal, C, Ada, and Modula-2) was a response.

Structured programming has evolved from three major ideas:

- A program should consist of modules that do simple things.
- These modules should access only the minimum amount of memory required to do their job.
- The written structure of a program should reflect its logical structure: no GOTO statements.

The simplicity and isolation of the modules has two advantages. First, a module of code can be tested before it is used, so building the program becomes akin to assembling a machine from stock parts, rather than carving it out of stone. Second, the isolation of the modules means that code can be reused in other programs without inadvertently altering memory in the new program. All experienced Pascal and C programmers have a "tool kit" of reuseable code for common tasks, and this tool kit greatly increases programmer productivity.

The absence of the GOTO statement—a very common statement in BASIC, FORTRAN, and COBOL—requires that the text of the program parallel the logic of the program. This makes the program easier to read and hence easier to debug and modify. It is no more difficult for a novice programmer to write a structured program than a nonstructured program, though programmers whose first language was BASIC initially find the transition difficult.

2. Incremental development. Don't try to write a large program in one step. Write the outlines first—the control and data structures—debug them, and test your ideas. Only then start filling in the outline. Program and debug in isolated modules whenever possible. Keep track of the time the program takes to run, and adjust it accordingly. If you try to write the program all at once, you risk obtaining something that is hopelessly slow. Modifying a functioning program is easier psychologically and allows you to experiment and detect error conditions.

3. Choose an appropriate language. Different problems require different tools. A large computer project may justify learning another language if that simplifies programming in the long run. BASIC, Pascal, and assembly language each have their advantages and disadvantages. Specialized languages are also helpful: APL is excellent for mathematical work; LISP is the standard for most artificial intelligence work, with PROLOG used in expert systems.

4. Figure out the I/O first. If a program uses data, figure out the file structures and I/O routines *first* and test out your ideas. File manipulation can make or break the speed of a program, and choosing the incorrect means of representing data can greatly complicate it. Data structures are half of program design. Become acquainted with various data structures—trees, arrays, graphs, records, and so forth—which have been developed by computer scientists; these are useful even if no I/O is involved. Properly designed file structures save time and memory.

5. Document extensively. Programs need to be documented extensively for your own benefit and the benefit of anyone else who might use the program. A line of documentation for every five lines of code is a good guideline. It is also helpful to keep a directory of variables and their uses, and provide an introduction describing the program, algorithms, and stating the date, purpose, and programmer. Documentation is critical for long-term maintenance: The amount that one forgets about program details in six months is phenomenal.

6. *Debug and test extensively.* Programs never work the first time. Some never work at all, but this can't be known without testing. Debugging is at least half of programming.

Debugging has been succinctly summarized as "make it run, make it right, make it rapid." First get the program running: Get the I/O working, the program doing some semblance of what it is supposed to be doing, and trap the obvious fatal errors. Second, check that the program is operating correctly—on numerical programs this may involve painstaking calculations unless you've got a mainframe program to check against, or can use published results, but always check. Finally, recoding may be needed to speed the program—in most programs 5% of the code accounts for 50% of the run time, and this code can be optimized for speed.

Debugging is simplified by structured programming. The most difficult bugs to track down are those that you could not imagine occurring, such as the change of variable values by a totally unrelated part of the program, or an unexpected branch. Neither should occur in a properly structured program.

7. *Recycle code.* Reusing old code is the key to programming productivity—don't rewrite code unless you have to. I often find it easier to modify an existing program when I set out to write a new one, even when the final version contains only one or two lines of the original. I suspect this is more comfortable because the old program provides a template of what needs to be done—initialization, error checking, input/output, and so forth—even when little actual code is reused.

Use published code. There are a variety of books along the lines of *Common BASIC Routines*, *Software Tools*, and so forth—it is a good idea to own a couple of these so you don't need to reinvent the wheel. Keeping a file of programs from computer magazines and other public-domain sources such as bulletin boards will also provide a variety of templates to follow when constructing new programs. Reading other programs provides ideas on improving your own, and keeps you up to date with current good programming practice.

8. *Watch round-off errors.* Round-off errors occur because computers keep track of only a finite number of digits in a numerical calculation. They are particularly problematic in statistical work where the terms in a single calculation may differ by several orders of magnitude. For example, the sum of squares of a series of numbers in the

100-1,000 range will quickly exceed the accuracy of a 32-bit floating point number, and subsequent small numbers added to that sum will be treated as if they were zero. This might show up as a negative variance or negative R-square but it might give results that are incorrect but not obviously in error. Accuracy in matrix inversion is also problematic. In many computer languages you can specify high-precision (e.g., 64-bit) arithmetic for critical calculations. This reduces round-off error to the levels found in mainframes but does not eliminate it.

9. *Watch the speed.* The worst time bandit is disk I/O, but this can often be minimized by careful data preparation. Frequently used numbers such as significance levels are more efficiently saved as arrays in RAM than read in or recomputed. Hard disks and RAM disks will also increase I/O speed. Customized data storage schemes that use binary images of data are much faster than ASCII storage.

Innocent-looking screen or printer I/O may also dramatically reduce the speed of a program. For example, this AppleSoft BASIC program

```
10   J = 2 : K = 3 : B = 2.5 : C = 3.067
20   FOR KA = 1 TO 500
30   I = J + K : A = B + C
40   PRINT A
50   PRINT "I EQUALS "; I
60   NEXT
```

runs in 21 seconds. Eliminating output statement 50 reduces the time to 16 seconds; eliminating both statements 50 and 40 reduces the time to 3 seconds.

There is usually a trade-off between *compiler* speed and *execution* speed—compilers that produce very fast code often take longer to do this. "Optimizing compilers" take key parts of the program (notably the insides of loops) and make them as fast as possible. Assembly language routines can be written for critical code if necessary.

Different implementations of the same language can differ substantially in speed. *Measure*—don't guess—the speeds of various instructions. When doing a major program with a new language or machine, I always time 10,000 iterations of common statements (e.g., IFs, arithmetic operations, array access, functions) with a stopwatch, and make a table of the relative speeds. Minor changes in statements can sometimes have dramatic impact on speed.

10. *Get it finished.* In the immortal words of Tom West, the project manager in Tracy Kidder's *Soul of a New Machine* (1982), "Not every-

thing worth doing is worth doing well." Any program can be improved—made faster, smaller, more flexible—but not every program deserves this treatment. Get it running and get it right, but know when to stop. The best program in the world is useless if it misses deadlines.

11. Program. The way to become a proficient programmer is to program. Programming is a craft that can be learned in a few hours but perfected only over a period of years. *Practice* is the key: The longer you program the better you will program.

Troubleshooting: Common Program Errors

Debugging the programs is a bit of an art, but a small number of errors account for a lot of the bugs. Be sure to check for the following:

Check the algorithm. Go through the malfunctioning part of the program step by step and make sure that the instructions you've coded actually do what you think they do. Remember the Hacker's Lament:

> I really hate this darn machine,
> I really wish they'd sell it.
> It never will do what I want,
> But only what I tell it.

Take a piece of paper, make a list of the variables, and go through the program instruction by instruction and check how the values change, or print out those variables at every point in the program. This is slow but it is the only way to check an algorithm.

Check initializations. When a program begins to run, all variables must be set to initial values. On some mainframes memory is initially set to zero; on most micros it is not. Failure to initialize usually results in strange results and/or "divide by zero" and "overflow" errors.

Check for infinite loops. If a program seems to do nothing and never stops, it is probably in an infinite loop. The most common cause of infinite loops is modifying a loop index inside a loop, for example:

```
100   FOR KA = 1 TO 10
   . . .
160   KA = KA – 1
   . . .
200   NEXT KA
```

In this example, KA is always reset to 1, and so the loop never finishes.

Occasionally an algorithm may seem to have an infinite loop when it is actually just working very slowly—get some idea of timing.

Use frequent output when debugging. Isolate the area where a program is misbehaving and output all relevant variables at every important step. This will usually locate the bug quickly. Some systems have a TRACE feature that does this automatically.

Check for duplicate variable names. Using the same name unintentionally for two variables creates all sorts of havoc. This is particularly a problem in complex programs and in unstructured programs.

Check for incorrect input. In a program processing data, make sure the input is correct before trying to correct the program: A perfectly good program will choke on bad data.

6. STATISTICS AND NUMERICAL PROCESSING

Overview

In the three years since the first edition of this book, the status of statistical analysis on PCs changed dramatically. In 1983 there were no serious comprehensive statistical packages for PCs. There are now a half dozen, including three of the major mainframe packages (SPSS, BMDP, and SAS). During that same period, the RAM available in most PCs expanded tenfold, and 10Mb hard disk drives became smaller and more affordable, so the differential between microcomputer and mainframe processing narrowed considerably. While the forte of the PC is still crunching text, not numbers, and for large-scale projects mainframe computers are superior, PC statistical packages can now handle many social science statistical projects.

A PC is no match against unlimited access to a mainframe, but usually mainframe access is limited. Time is constrained by Kafkaesque accounting schemes, memory limited except during off-hours, and a time-shared mainframe is often as slow as a PC. A PC is small, but consistent; PC software is frequently better integrated and more "user friendly" than mainframe software; and PCs have better graphics capabilities than most mainframe terminals. Finally , many data sets do not require the resources of a mainframe.

This chapter will focus on comprehensive statistical packages (CSPs) such as SPSS that have extensive facilities for data entry, editing, and transformation, and contain the full panoply of statistical routines including descriptive statistics, basic graphs and plots, regression and correlation, analysis of variance, contingency tables, and multivariate techniques such as factor analysis, MANOVA, and discriminant analysis. Most of what is said about CSPs also applies to specialized statistical programs such as advanced econometrics software.

Introduction: Micros Versus Mainframes

Microcomputers have already replaced mainframes in all but the most complex word processing applications, and are sufficient for most small-business accounting applications. This section will focus on the relative merits of PCs and mainframes in numerical processing, with an emphasis on statistical analysis.

Six factors affect the relative strength of PCs and mainframes in statistical research: speed, accuracy, memory, software, data, graphics, and user cost. A mainframe is superior to the PC on all but one factor, but in a time-shared environment the PC begins to catch up.

Speed. PCs differ by a factor of ten or more in speed, and differences in the implementation of software can raise that difference to a factor of fifty. Numerical coprocessors for floating point (decimal) arithmetic dramatically speed up the execution of statistical programs and are virtually required for some statistical packages. At the moment the fastest commercially available PCs—for example, machines based on the Intel 80386 or Motorola 68020 chips with numerical coprocessors— are only half as slow as many mainframes and will easily run faster in terms of wristwatch time than a time-shared mainframe. In contrast, an older, slower machine such as a Z80-based CP/M computer or 6502-based Apple II will be abysmally slow and impractical for all but the smallest problems.

Most university mainframes, meanwhile, are effectively slowed by time-sharing, perhaps among hundreds of users. De facto speed becomes a function of the load on the machine: A program that takes one clock minute to run at 3:00 a.m. during vacation might take ten clock minutes at 3:00 p.m. the week before classes end. A heavy time-sharing load can easily slow a mainframe to the speed of a fast PC.

Accuracy. There is no intrinsic difference in the accuracy of micros and mainframes—while mainframes have greater accuracy per computer word, micros store numbers in several words to obtain comparable accuracy. An 8-bit micro may use 32-bit or 64-bit arithmetic. However, as accuracy increases the speed of computation decreases and memory requirements increase.

All numerical programs must deal with "round-off error," which occurs because computers have only finite numerical accuracy, and many nonrepeating decimal fractions are repeating binary fractions (e.g., 0.1). Round-off error is a major problem in statistical routines, where large sums, sums of squares, and complex calculations such as matrix inversion may exceed the internal accuracy of the machine and the components of a calculation may differ by many orders of magnitude. Good statistical software *must* be written specifically to alleviate round-off problems—standard mathematical operations alone are not sufficient.

Memory. Most CSPs require at least 400K of RAM and recommend having as much RAM as the machine can normally handle. Even with this memory, PC statistical packages rely heavily on disk storage and are *much* easier to use if a hard disk is available. All CSPs require multiple disks for the program and additional disks for data: A hard disk eliminates a lot of time-consuming and aggravating disk swapping. A PC that is perfectly satisfactory for word processing may require substantial additional hardware in the form of RAM and disk capacity to be suitable for efficient statistical analysis on large data sets.

Software. Statistical software for PCs is now equal to that of mainframes and, in fact, often uses the same FORTRAN code. Most of the major mainframe statistical packages are now available on the IBM PC, and high-quality packages are also available for the Macintosh, CP/M, and UNIX machines. In addition to the CSPs, an assortment of specialized packages is available in the fields of statistical graphics, computer-assisted interviewing, and advanced econometric modeling.

CSP programs differ somewhat in accuracy, particularly on data sets containing high levels of multicollinearity, so it is wise to check this carefully. Computer publications such as *Byte* and *Social Science Microcomputer Review* periodically do comparative evaluations of programs for speed, capacity, and accuracy.

CSPs are still relatively expensive as PC programs go, costing between $400 and $1,500 at the moment. However, most firms selling CSPs are providing site license agreements to reduce the unit cost when a number of copies of the program are used at an institution. For example, at Northwestern the $600 Systat package costs only $100 if purchased under the university's site license agreement. Specialized packages are less expensive, usually around $50-$150. Because of the meticulous programming and error checking required in statistical programming, public-domain software should probably not be relied upon, and very little such software is available in any case.

Graphics. This is the one area where PCs outshine most mainframes. The average PC has far superior graphics than the average time-shared terminal, and few mainframe CSPs will work with graphics terminals. A PC-driven dot-matrix printer can be used to dump graphics at a fraction of the cost, and far greater convenience, than a mainframe plotter, and with higher precision than a text terminal. Some PC CSPs will work with plotters, or at least can transfer data to a business graphics program that can use a plotter.

Cost. A typical statistical computing project will consume somewhere between $100 and $1,000 worth of computer time. If the data need substantial cleaning the cost can be much greater. In the good old days of computer "funny money"—when computing time was available in surplus—funding statistical projects was not much of a problem. In the recession-plagued 1980s it can be a problem. In most universities a certain amount of mainframe computer time is available without cost. Problems arise when that money is exhausted: At more than one installation, the money spent just to complete a mainframe computer project would buy a PC customized for numerical processing and the appropriate software.

PCs reduce risk. Research is necessarily unpredictable, and there is nothing more frustrating than running out of computer funds in the middle of a project—additional tests are not done, errors are not corrected, a slipshod job is done when additional computer money alone would increase quality. Once the data have been cleaned and prepared, and the programs written, the analysis itself is almost trivial in terms of labor, but costly in terms of computer time. In mainframe computing, the amount of analysis accomplished is frequently a function of the money left in the budget. Hence one gets beer-budget statistical analysis on champagne-budget data.

On a PC additional analysis requires only a trivial investment in electricity, plus time. Techniques that are prohibitively expensive in terms of CPU time—probit analysis, nonlinear curve fitting, multiple controls—can be used without putting the project budget in jeopardy. This in turn increases productivity—it is far more comfortable to work knowing that a mistake means only lost time, and not a lost opportunity to do additional tests. When it is possible to make mistakes, rather than insisting on perfection the first time through, an analyst can do the exploration and experimentation that is the mark of good statistical work.

The upshot of this is the following. PCs are slower than mainframes, though not by a lot. With proper software they are just as accurate.

Current floppy disks restrict samples sizes to somewhere in the neighborhood of 1,000-3,000 cases, depending on the machine, though that can be extended substantially with a hard disk. Good comprehensive statistical packages cost over $500, which means that they have a higher initial cost compared to mainframe computing, but their operating cost is essentially zero. If you can operate within those restrictions, use the PC—otherwise, stick with the mainframe.

Operating: Data Preparation

Exactly how many data can a statistics program handle? Again, the constraints involve software as much as hardware. A typical 5-inch floppy disk will hold around 300K bytes and, figuring the equivalent of two punch cards of data per case, yields a maximum sample of around 1,800. Newer floppy disks hold as much as 1,200K, which increases capacity considerably. As a general rule of thumb, any sample under 1,500 can be analyzed on a PC; over 3,000 probably is better on the mainframe; and sizes in between depend on the program. If you have a hard disk very large files can be analyzed, though processing time may be slow.

Preprocessing data on a mainframe may save considerable time and space. If a data set contains 200 variables but your study requires only 20, reduce it to the information you need, perhaps do some cleaning and transformations (e.g., with SPSS then a WRITE VARS) and only then download to the micro for intensive analysis.

Many researchers find PCs cost-effective for data entry, provided a sufficient number of machines are available. A data-base management program or specialized computer-assisted interviewing (CAI) programs can check the validity of data as they are being entered—for example, recognizing when a value is out of range or a letter is entered where a number is expected—and thus are far more likely to yield error-free data than traditional methods using coding sheets, keypunching, and manual verification.

CAI programs are usually used in telephone interviews. The CAI program displays the questions to be asked, and the interviewer enters answers directly into the PC, where they are checked for errors on entry. CAI systems can handle complex questionnaires with various question contingencies, automatically randomize the use and ordering of questions, and reduce the amount of training required of interviewers. Because data are entered at the time the interview is being conducted, they are available for analysis almost immediately.

The long-term prospect for data storage on micros is bright due to the development of optical storage technology and, in the short term, the mass production of hard disks. In five years it will probably be practical to distribute very large data sets such as census data, international event data, and national election survey data in a medium that can be analyzed directly by a PC. The commercial demands by business for this type of capacity encourage its development, and the social science researcher will be a beneficiary.

Operation: PC Statistical Packages

At the present time, two statistical packages dominate social science PC computing: SPSS/PC and Systat. Both are comprehensive packages offering a full range of contemporary statistical methods. Both can be run either interactively or in a "batch" mode; both can read and write ASCII files; both provide reasonably good on-line help to the user; both have good error checking and error recovery. Both, alas, are copy-protected. I am currently writing a primer on Systat and am thus more acquainted with it, though I've used SPSS extensively on mainframes in the past. This evaluation is based on the software available in September 1986; both SPSS, Inc., and Systat, Inc., are working on significant enhancements to their products that will be available by the time this book appears.

SPSS/PC+ is a major subset of the popular mainframe statistical package SPSS-X. Since most social scientists are initially trained on SPSS, almost no additional training is required to use the package. SPSS documentation is exceptionally good, and SPSS, Inc., has produced a variety of primers and manuals suited for different audiences. On the down side, SPSS/PC+ preserves the antiquated command structure of SPSS-X, the system has no significant time-series analysis capabilities (e.g., ARIMA models or autocorrelation), and the system runs only on MS-DOS machines.

Systat (Version 3.0) runs on all major PC operating systems (CP/M, MS-DOS, Unix, the Macintosh, and VAX) and covers the same statistical techniques as SPSS/PC+ with the addition of time-series analysis. It has proven to be one of the most accurate of all statistical packages, micro or mainframe, and it contains an extensive BASIC programming language for data transformation. Systat's command structure is quite different from SPSS's (it is similar to that of SAS) and requires additional learning for most social scientists, though having used both I much prefer the SAS/Systat approach. On the down side, Systat is highly modular and requires a lot of disk swapping if used without a hard disk, the manual is written for the professional social statistician rather than the beginner, and the graphics capabilities are limited.

In addition to SPSS and Systat, the mainframe programs BMDP

and SAS are available in relatively complete PC versions for MS-DOS machines, though their price ($1,500 and up for the complete package, according to *Info World*, September 1, 1986) is prohibitive. MINITAB is supposed to become available soon, though I've yet to see it, and the econometric time-series packages TSP and RATS are available in MS-DOS versions. At the present time Systat is the only CSP available for the Macintosh, though the STATVIEW package contains most routines except multivariate statistics (other than regression) and time-series analysis. The situation on the Mac is likely to change dramatically in the next couple of years, and some specialized programs are available that make extensive use of Macintosh graphics.

Troubleshooting: Evaluating Statistics Packages

In general, the advice on statistics packages is "ask someone who uses one," with the additional proviso of checking accuracy. In the event that you are evaluating a new package here are some key things to watch for:

• Check the basic constraints of the program—how many cases will it handle and how many variables per case? Also get some sense of speed—create a fake file (a big fake file) and run a regression or cross-tabs on it. Programs and routines differ substantially in the amount of time they require. Also check how much time you spend swapping disks.

• How well does the program handle cross-tabulation? What is the maximum sample size? How deep can controls be nested? Crosstabs appear to be the Achilles heel of microcomputer packages because they have a prodigious appetite for memory, are not used in the physical and biological sciences, use weird nonparametric statistics, and in general challenge the skill of the system designer far more than regression or t-tests. If a program has a weak point, it is likely to be in cross-tabulation.

• How well does the program handle missing data? This facility is another glaring weakness in many programs. SPSS set a high standard for the ease and flexibility of handling missing data, but don't automatically expect to find that in other programs.

• It is almost essential that the statistical program be able to read and write an ASCII text file. ASCII text is inefficient computationally, so most programs use their own formats for data storage. But be sure it is *possible* to use ASCII, since this will allow the transfer of data between machines. Some specialized programs allow data to be entered only through the program's editor, which makes it impossible to transfer data without retyping it.

It is *very* helpful if the statistics program can easily share data with a word-processor and business graphics program. Simple business graphics are useful for exploratory data analysis; interface with a word processor simplifies the incorporation of results into manuscripts.

• Check the documentation and formatting of the output. Is the output unambiguous? Are standard statistical abbreviations used and located in reasonable places? Can the output be easily dumped to the printer? Is the documentation readable? Do the authors appear to know statistics, or did they take this project on after finishing a word processing system? All of the successful mainframe packages were written by working statisticians, not by idle programmers, and the same will undoubtedly be true in micros.

• Programs should be benchmarked for accuracy. Always. I don't trust my own programs—I'm hardly going to trust one written by a stranger. If you are buying a program, insist on seeing tests benchmarked against Systat or an accurate mainframe package. Many packages now include this as part of their documentation. In any case, it is a good idea to cross-check part of your data against the system it is replacing until you are confident of the program. Statistical programming is notoriously sensitive to minor errors—a plus or minus sign, reversed subscripts, forgetting to reinitialize sums—that are not caught as compiler errors and only randomly cause problems in execution, and may even work most of the time, so *be very careful!*

• Check the command structure of the program. Menu-driven programs are easier to use at first, but become awkward as you become more experienced. For serious analysis, command-driven programs (the norm in mainframes and PC CSPs) are preferable. It is very helpful to be able to run a program in "batch" mode, setting up a series of commands that will run unattended. The slower speed of a PC is less of a constraint when an analysis can be done without the researcher present.

• How well does the program use the graphics capabilities of your computer? A statistical program should make extensive use of PC graphics capabilities—it is often far easier to see a relationship than to read it. Also be sure that the program can easily produce printed output on the equipment you currently own.

7. OTHER SOFTWARE

Overview

Word processing, programming, and statistical analysis are the most common uses of PCs in the social science environment. These applications represent only a small fraction of the software that is available, however. This chapter will briefly discuss other software that is likely to be of use to a social scientist.

Generally, there are three sources of software. The first, and most common, is commercial software, which can cost anywhere between $20 and $800, should be thoroughly debugged and tested, and should have professionally written documentation. At the other end of the spectrum is public-domain software, which is available for free through bulletin boards and users' groups, is usually written by amateurs, is frequently not completely debugged, and rarely has much documentation. An intermediate and increasing popular source of software is "shareware": software that is freely distributed through bulletin boards with a request that the user send a modest amount (usually $10 to $50) in exchange for more complete documentation and notices about program upgrades.

Ironically, price and source provide almost no indication of software quality. Small firms have produced commercial software and shareware that costs a fraction of the price of major products and yet performs better. Similarly, only a few large firms have *consistently* produced quality products—MicroSoft and Borland International are almost unique in this regard. Many firms that have produced excellent software in one area or for one machine have produced junk when they tried to expand. Above all, do not rely on advertising: Many firms advertise "vaporware" (so called because it is less corporeal than hardware or software): mythical products with mythical features and imaginative delivery dates ("Real Soon Now," in Jerry Pournell's phrase) which often as not never come to pass. A bird in the hand is better than a ghost in the bush.

There is one and only one source of reliable information about software: word of mouth, which includes friends, independent users' groups, and reliable journalistic reviews. All commercial software goes through extensive "beta-testing" by users, and by the time it is available for purchase it should have a known track record in the specialized magazines and among users' groups.

Spreadsheets

A spreadsheet is a table of numbers and other information that has computational instructions programmed into it by the user. For example, a typical spreadsheet might contain grades for a class. Each row of the spreadsheet would be a student; the columns would contain grades for various assignments. The final column in each row could be the average grade for each student, and the final row in each column could contain the average for each assignment. When any entry in the table is changed—for example, if a student turns in a late assignment and changes a zero to some other grade—then the averages are recomputed automatically.

In addition to allowing simple arithmetic operations, sophisticated spreadsheets provide a number of statistical and economic functions (e.g., discounting), can do a variety of logical operations, and have considerable flexibility in formatting output. Because spreadsheets can sort on alphabetic as well as numeric information, they are useful in a number of small data-base applications. Spreadsheets range in price from about $50 for the simplest to $300-$500 for complex integrated spreadsheets.

While the original concept of the spreadsheet came from business accounting, the concept is very general and lends itself to innumerable applications. The best way to illustrate this is simply to list the tasks I've used spreadsheets for during the past year:

- keeping track of applicants for a departmental position so they could be easily sorted by specialization and rank
- several grant proposal budgets
- minor statistical analyses for conference papers, along with generating statistical graphics for the papers
- analyzing the graduate program with respect to class sizes, qualifying exam interest, and job placement
- analyzing demand of teaching assistants by class size and doing a comparative analysis with other departments
- recording and computing class grades

Plus, in non-work-related endeavors

- household budget
- financial forecasting for my brother's small winery in conjunction with a bank loan application
- wonderful, wild, and wacky IRS Form 1040, particularly the business expenses on Schedule C
- and, finally, checkbook balancing, for which I once swore I'd never use a computer but which is well worth the effort in time saved

Almost any small data project, whether numerical or nonnumerical, can be usefully done on a good spreadsheet—it is a general utility program on par with the word processor.

I would *not* advise using a spreadsheet to do complicated statistical analyses such as linear regression, though some books suggest this. Spreadsheets are not designed with the complex error checking of a statistical package such as BMDP or Systat and, while they will usually function without problems, you have no guarantees. For advanced statistical work, use a statistical program.

Integrated spreadsheet programs combine a spreadsheet with some other applications—usually business graphics and data-base functions, though some of the more elaborate integrated systems incorporate telecommunications, word processing, and other functions as well. The most popular spreadsheets on the IBM PC and Macintosh—Lotus 1-2-3 and MicroSoft Excel, respectively—are integrated. The advantage of an integrated spreadsheet is that one can switch between common tasks such as manipulating data and graphing it without leaving the program. The disadvantage is that the features in the integrated program may be inferior to those available in independent programs. The tendency at the moment is to integrate some applications but not all, and leave most of the data exchange to the operating systems.

Sophisticated spreadsheets such as Lotus and Excel allow one to create "macros," which are essentially memorized sets of keystrokes. Suppose, for example, that in a gradesheet you decided to allow some students to drop the lowest of five grades and then recompute the average on the basis of the remaining grades. Rather than doing these operations individually, you could create a macro that would change a grade to zero, then go to the end of the row and change the formula from dividing the sum of the grades by 5 to dividing by 4. For each grade dropped this macro would be invoked with one or two keystrokes rather than the dozen or so required to do the operation manually. Macros are complicated to set up but save significant amounts of time (as well as reducing the probability of errors) when a number of repetitive operations need to be done.

Data-Base Management Programs

In the early days of the personal computer a widely suggested use for the new machines was the maintenance of recipe files and phone lists. While both tasks are more efficiently done with a fifty-cent box of 3×5 index cards, they are a simple example of what quickly became a major use of PCs: the data-base management systems, or DBMS.

A data base (DB) is simply a collection of information. Data bases in business include payroll, accounts receivable, mailing lists, and inventories; in the social sciences a data base might be a bibliography, notes, biographical information, experiment results, census tract data, or a file of cultural characteristics. The advantage of a computerized data base over a set of note cards is that a PC can manipulate the file—for example, sorting it, changing it, or quickly finding items within it. For example, at one major social science journal, the time required to prepare the yearly index was reduced from one week to a half hour by the conversion of all of the journal records to a Condor DBMS system running on a lowly Apple II.

Relational DBMS are the most popular type of advanced DBMS for microcomputers. These allow logical and mathematical operations to be done on an entire file and can create new sets of data out of combinations of existing records. For example, a file of authors of books on urban crime written after 1970 could be merged with a file containing the works those same authors wrote prior to 1970 to ascertain the backgrounds of writers on urban crime in the 1970s. Many relational DBMS can effectively be used as specialized programming languages for information manipulation and file management. In many cases it is far easier to write a file management program in a relational DBMS than it is to write that same program in a general-purpose language such as BASIC or Pascal.

DBMS vary substantially in speed. Working with a large set of data almost requires a hard disk and even with a hard disk an operation such as a sort or an index can take hours for a large file. Ease of data entry and modification is another important feature; *error checking* on entry is very helpful and reduces subsequent data cleaning costs. It should be possible to *restructure* the record format without having to reenter the data. Most research data bases require restructuring sooner or later, and most DBMS allow this, but not all. Flexible output, including ASCII file transfers, report generators, and business graphics capabilities, are very useful.

A type of DBMS that is particularly useful in research involving documents is the "full-text data base." These data bases hold a document, or series of documents, and all important words (e.g., words other than *a*, *and*, *the*, and so forth) are indexed. By constructing complex queries, it is possible to retrieve quickly, for example, all references to "pets" in a series of transcripts of divorce cases. The size of the document is usually limited only by the disk space available for the document and index; indexing a large document can take hours (though this is done automatically and does not require attention), but retrieval is done in seconds. The "Nota Bene" full-text system by Dragonfly Software has become particularly popular in this genre.

Statistical and Business Graphics

Microcomputers can be used to produce charts and graphs quickly. "Business graphics" programs produce pie charts, bar charts, and a variety of line charts from data entered directly or transferred from a spreadsheet or DBMS program. Most business graphics programs cannot produce that mainstay of social science research, the bivariate scattergram, and for that specialized statistical graphics programs are used.

Statistical graphics is a very hot topic among statisticians at the moment, so some of these programs provide very creative means of data display not discussed in the average statistics book. For example, there are now programs that will produce tables of scattergrams, allowing one to study two nominal and two interval variables simultaneously. A recent program developed for the Macintosh, MacSpin, generates a three-dimensional scattergram that can be rotated and examined from any angle, thus displaying three interval variables.

The use of color in graphical displays is another place where microcomputers have an edge over mainframes, though this use is sometimes controversial. *Properly* used, color can add additional dimensions to a data display. Color is particularly effective is displaying geographical data, where two dimensions are already occupied by the map of the data itself; color provides a third (or more) dimension for displaying data. A number of map-oriented programs are available. Improperly used, color is simply distracting and makes the data more difficult to interpret. Other disadvantages to color are that expensive specialized plotters are needed to produce hard copy and that output cannot be reproduced except with color duplication processes.

Graphics programs range from public domain and shareware programs costing zero to tens of dollars to statistical graphics programs costing in the hundreds of dollars. While most good programs support a variety of color graphics cards, printers, and plotters, it is wise to check on compatibility before buying. Compatibility is particularly problematic in the case of high-resolution color graphics, where the "standards" seem to change annually.

RAM-Resident Utilities

There are a large number of compact programs that allow one to do small tasks such as take notes, consult a clock or calendar, do calculations, consult an address book, use a modem, or even play a game of "Break-Out" while briefly interrupting other programs. These are called "RAM-resident" utilities on MS-DOS machines, since they reside in memory; on the Macintosh they are called "desk accessories" and reside on the system disk. All of these programs are relatively inexpensive and allow one to customize the operating environment. Borland International's "Sidekick" program (and its equivalents) are very popular on the MS-DOS machines; Macintosh desk accessories are widely available through bulletin boards and users' groups on a "shareware" basis.

RAM-resident programs occupy memory and may reduce the effectiveness of other programs, and in some combinations have caused the operating system to crash. As a consequence, the current vogue is the creation of RAM-resident programs to manage other RAM-resident programs.

Disk and File Utilities

Disk utility programs are predominantly used to copy "copy-protected" disks, either onto another disk or onto a hard disk. Provided the copying program is more sophisticated than the copy-protection scheme, the copy will be as good as the original.

Copy-protection is a bit of silliness left over from the early days of microcomputing when the market for programs was small and program producers had visions of massive sales being lost to software pirates. The producers may or may not have been correct: Software piracy clearly exists, but it is less certain how many people with pirated copies would have bought the programs (particularly nongame programs). My own attitude as both a consumer and a producer of software is simple: I do not produce copy-protected software, and I buy it only when the program is outstanding, reasonably priced, and there is no alternative. Systat and MicroSoft's Excel are the only copy-protected products I've bought, and shortly after I purchased Excel, MicroSoft removed the protection. Since a number of consumers and producers have a similar policy, copy-protection is beginning to disappear from the scene.

File utility programs allow one to recover information that has been accidentally deleted through user or machine error. Because hardware errors occur to even the most careful user—and user errors occur to the rest of us—these programs are essential. In almost all cases, short of the physical destruction or reformatting of the disk, most of a text file can be reconstructed with a file recovery program. The amount of effort and knowledge involved varies with the system—and it may take an hour or more to do the job—but with a file utility you at least have the option.

The "Norton Utilities" are the standard for the IBM PC; a number of public-domain utilities exist for the Mac, as well as the commercial MacTools. These programs cost around $50.

Troubleshooting

As noted above, the best way to avoid problems with software is to buy programs that other people recommend and are using. A few helpful words from an experienced user can save hours of frustration with a program. Beyond that, here are a few bits of advice.

Ease of use and learning. Studies have found that up to 80% of the total cost of using software is involved in *training.* Over time and multiple users, training costs become larger than the purchase cost of the hardware and software. While academic users do not have quite the personnel turnover of business nor the funds to buy the best programs, it is still important to remember that time invested in learning to use a program, and teaching others to use it, is a *real cost*: $50 saved on a cheap but laboriously difficult program is $50 wasted on lost time.

Ease of use is particularly important for programs that are complicated and used infrequently since the program will have to be re-learned several times. A good program should be usable with just a few minutes of review and a reference card. Early microcomputer programs were notoriously difficult to learn—witness the number of books about WordStar compared to those about MacWrite—but things have improved dramatically over the past few years.

While any program should be easy to use, there is still a relationship between the capabilities of a program and the complexity of learning it. Powerful programs require more training and documentation than simple ones. Professionally written documentation, with lots of examples, is a must. Since documentation must be directed at three very different user communities—the beginner, the experienced "power" user, and the experienced casual user—many complex programs now provide multiple manuals.

The tendency of most programs is to be underutilized: Most are capable of doing far more than they are used for. The secret to getting the full potential out of a program has been enshrined in the acronym RYFM, which, for public consumption, may be translated as "Read your fact-filled manual." In numerous cases the apparent weaknesses of a program may be resolvable by well-documented features of the program. RYFM applies particularly to Macintosh users, who rarely if ever read manuals and depend on word of mouth, instinct, and help files to learn how to use programs.

Capacity. Two otherwise equivalent programs may differ by a factor of ten or more in their maximum record size and number of records that can be stored per disk. There is usually a trade-off between speed and capacity—programs that use disk space most efficiently require more time. Some programs manage to be poor on both dimensions.

Data I/O. Getting data in and out of programs can be a major headache at times and is worth serious consideration. There are a variety of standard data exchange formats and two suitably complicated programs can usually exchange data, but much work can be saved by getting compatible programs. If a program can read and write ASCII files, you are usually safe, and this also allows data to be downloaded from mainframes.

A current common problem is exchanging data between IBM PCs and Macintoshes. In a university environment the easiest way to do this is upload the data in ASCII form from one machine into a mainframe, then download into the other machine. This takes only a modem and some telecommunications software. With appropriate programs two machines can also be connected directly via a "null modem" (the ImageWriter printer cable on the Mac is a null modem) and ASCII files exchanged thusly. There are also some direct hardware solutions for this, but at the moment they are quite expensive.

Support. In the software business, the word *support* refers to the extent to which you can get help with the software. Here are four sources of support, in increasing order of cost and decreasing reliability. The cheapest and most reliable, as always, is *friends* who are also using the same software; local users' groups can also provide information. The next best are well-written *books* on the software—mass-distribution bookstores such as Waldenbooks and B. Dalton carry a variety of books (usually $15-$30) on popular software. Magazine subscriptions also help in this regard.

If you buy software locally, the *dealer* might be able to help, but don't count on it. Computer dealers have a very difficult time keeping knowledgeable help and hence they are likely to know only a few programs. You pay for this support, of course, in higher prices for the software. Lastly and leastly, some *manufacturers* provide telephone support. If this is free (800 numbers) you can count on waiting forever before you get through the busy signals; alternatively, the manufacturer may charge a fee for telephone consultation. The exception to this rule is small companies, where you may well end up talking with the programmer.

Compatibility with peripherals. The final issue to look for is compatibility of your software with the equipment your own. Not all programs work with all equipment, and you should be particularly careful on compatibility with the following:

- unusual computers, particularly some of the early "IBM-compatibles" and esoteric CP/M machines
- hard disk drives, particularly large ones
- high-resolution color graphics cards
- expansion RAM—the program may not be able to use all of the memory of your machine
- printers, particularly laser printers and any older printer
- mice and graphics tablets

This looks like a long list, and it is: Compatibility should never be assumed, only tested.

8. GRAPHICS

From almost their first introduction, PCs have had exceptional graphics capabilities. Just as the seemingly simple spreadsheet program VisiCalc paved the way to large memories and integrated programs, so the seemingly insatiable drive to blast away at little creatures marching across the video screen led to the development of graphics capabilities unmatched by the average mainframe terminal.

Graphics production on a PC provides at least three advantages over pen and ink. First, a PC can produce very high precision (1/100 inch [0.25 mm]) statistical graphics in very little time and for virtually no cost. Second, in freehand drawing, the machine provides a facility for erasing and reusing graphic elements that is difficult to obtain in any other medium. Finally, animation is trivially easy on a microcomputer, and very difficult in any other medium. The disadvantages of computer graphics are the equipment and expense required to generate color and shading, and an interface between visual thought and visible copy considerably more complex than that of the hand-held pen.

Paradoxically, good graphics can be produced on even the least expensive home computer, but excellent graphics require phenomenally expensive hardware and sophisticated software. Fifty dollars will give you Space Invaders-quality animation, but $5,000 is required to achieve the color, resolution, and shading of a $.50 box of crayons. This section will focus only on the capabilities of systems that cost less than $1,000.

Introduction: How Graphics Work

To understand the limitations of computer graphics, it is helpful to have some idea of how they work. All microcomputer graphics are done in terms of "pixels"—a single point of color. Resolution is determined by the dimensions of the grid of pixels; this is typically 600 wide by 400 high, but varies substantially between machines. Graphics displays are usually "bit-mapped," which means that for every pixel there are bits somewhere in memory determining pixel color. With bit-mapping, changing the graphics display is simply a matter of rewriting parts of memory, which can be done very quickly.

Since there are a finite number of pixels, any drawing is approximate. Lines at some angles will appear very jagged, circles are uneven, and letters are made up of a series of dots. For high-resolution screens this is not very noticeable, but on low-resolution screens it can become quite annoying, particularly when the screen is enlarged.

Most PCs use primarily monochrome (black-and-white) graphics. Color requires additional memory or else results in lower resolution, and good color monitors are expensive. Odd color effects that look nice in Space Invaders become nauseating in word processing. Consequently, most PCs require special peripheral boards for color, which provide high resolution with a broad range of colors (frequently 256 or more) when displayed on a high-quality monitor.

Graphics programming is relatively simple, and almost all PC programming languages have simple graphics commands for drawing straight lines, changing pixels, and writing text. For example, the plot of a sine curve in AppleSoft Basic requires only

```
20 HGR : HCOLOR = 7
30 HPLOT 0,100
40 FOR KA = 0 TO 278
50 HPLOT TO KA, 100 + 50 * SIN(KA * 10)
60 NEXT
```

Some languages have commands for automatically drawing geometric figures and for color filling. Simple graphics can be incorporated into a program with a minimum of additional trouble. Animation is done by simply drawing and erasing a figure in quick succession.

Operation: Graphics Software

There are two general types of graphics software. Statistical graphics programs take numerical information and convert it to a graphical display with little or no additional drawing by the user. These are very efficient for displaying statistical results but can produce only a limited set of displays. Graphics editors and graphics programming, in contrast, give the computerized equivalent of freehand drawing and may be used to create any graphics material.

STATISTICAL GRAPHICS

There are a large number of programs for creating statistical graphics—e.g., pie charts and various three-dimensional plots. These are usually called "business graphics" to distinguish them from animation and engineering graphics packages.

The two key features to check in a business graphics package are the data editor and the labeling. It should be possible to be able to edit and scale information after entry so that the resulting plot appears as you would like it, not just as the program would like. Graphics program integration with editors, statistical programs, and DBMS is helpful. A graph is rarely satisfactory the first time through, so good editing capabilities and ease of data input are important. Finally, it is frequently useful to be able to create "overlays," where two different graphs are superimposed for comparison purposes.

Many programs restrict the size and location of labels. Choose a program with labeling that corresponds to your esthetic preferences, or use a graphics editor to modify the screen later. Advertised examples—usually an optimistic line graph showing the developer's software overtaking all competitors—are frequently the *best* that the program can manage, not the average. Caveat emptor.

Most, but not all, business graphics programs can at least print graphics on a printer, and some will also output to a plotter. Not all programs work with all printers, so check this feature. Unless color printing facilities are available, color is usually best avoided in graphics that are intended for publication. A chart that looks fine in color may be far less clear in monochrome. On many machines, color results in reduced resolution. In place of color, monochrome "shading" can be used by many programs.

In addition to business graphics, almost all statistical packages have some high-resolution graphics capabilities; the better packages use graphics extensively. In the long term, these facilities should have a major impact on the presentation of statistical results, since it is usually easier to look at a chart than to look at tables. Specialized programs that can produce statistical graphics involving maps simplify the presentation of geographical data, and can present a very large amount of information in a small area when color is used.

GRAPHICS EDITORS

A general graphics editor changes graphics as a text editor changes text, modifying anything on the graphics screen and allowing alteration of labels, shading, and so forth. The MacPaint and MacDraw programs for the Macintosh are the best known of this genre. There are a variety of stand-alone programs for freehand drawing and animation; these are particularly helpful in line drawing and color filling. Generally computer graphics are more difficult to create than pencil or ink drawing. They are advantageous only if a drawing is to be slightly modified and reused several times, or if the machine has already done much of the drawing.

Computer-aided design (CAD) programs are an advanced form of graphics editor used in mechanical drawing. Advanced CAD programs have the ability, for example, to convert a plane drawing into a three-dimensional drawing, rotate the drawing, rescale it, and so forth. The best CAD programs require very expensive ($20,000) hardware and high-resolution display screens, but a large number of good programs ($200-$2,000, depending on features) are available for PCs.

Operation: Graphics Input

Graphics input is a more difficult problem than it first appears, because the relatively low resolution and monochrome screen exaggerates errors that would not be noticed in a freehand ink drawing. Graphics can be entered freehand through a cursor or with a tracing device, camera, or graphics terminal emulator.

CURSOR DRAWING

Freehand drawing is most commonly done with a mouse. This looks easy but requires practice: Drawing with a mouse has been compared to drawing with a bar of soap. The key to good drawings is ample use of the enlarged picture (called "Fitbits" in MacPaint), where pixels can be manipulated individually. The best freehand drawings are of very high quality: The limitations are in the skill of the operator, not the machine.

TRACING DEVICES

These are devices that sense the location of a pointer in two dimensions, and with proper software that location is used to control the screen cursor. Light pens ($300-$700) appear to draw directly on the screen (in fact, there is a complicated software interface); they are widely used in advanced graphics systems but are limited in PCs due to low reliability, expense, and a poor software base. A graphics tablet ($400-$1000) is a panel that responds to an electronic pen. It has high resolution and is particularly useful for tracing images such as maps or diagrams. Freehand drawing is possible with practice. A touch pad ($80-$150) is similar to a graphics tablet, but uses touch as the location sensor and has considerably lower resolution.

DIGITIZERS AND CAMERAS

A digitizer scans a document and converts it into pixels; a typical application is converting a photograph into a computer graphic that can be inserted into a document. Digitizers such as the Thunderscan for the Macintosh use the printer to position and move the document being scanned and are thus relatively inexpensive ($150-$300).

Cameras based on solid-state technology are available for $200-$700. The less expensive versions are monochrome; more expensive ones will handle gray tones. By placing filters in front of the lens, color can be approximated. Cameras require some clever programming and experimentation to function well, but the field is quickly developing. In assessing whether a camera will work, keep in mind that in PC cameras, as in biological sight, the steps of detecting light, motion, shape, and color are progressively more difficult.

GRAPHICS-TERMINAL-EMULATING PROGRAMS

With appropriate software (see Chapter 9), many PCs can emulate, with some loss of resolution, a mainframe graphics terminal. This allows the sophisticated graphics software of a mainframe to be used to create an initial image, which can then be edited or saved on disk.

Operation: Graphics Output

Getting graphics into some "hard" form is less complicated than input, paticularly since dot-matrix printers are widely available. These require a printer graphics-dump program ($20-$50) or a printer interface designed to dump graphics on command ($80-$150). As always, there must be a proper match between the computer, interface, software, and printer. Graphics dumps are possible with impact printers but the results are less precise.

Most graphics-dump programs can do some transformation of the screen; rotations, inverse (black to white and vice versa), enlargement, and cropping are the most common facilities. The aspect ratio—the ratio of height to width of a pixel—of printer and screen graphics is frequently different, so some experimentation may be necessary in order to get a plot that looks as nice on paper as it does on the screen.

The resolution of most dot-matrix printers is on the order of 1/100th of an inch in both vertical and horizontal directions, finer than most human drafting, though not as fine as some mainframe plotters. Since a 400 × 200 pixel screen on 8.5 × 11 inch paper uses only 1/30th inch resolution, printers are capable of considerably better resolution than most screens. Many graphics programs can exploit the full precision of printers and will print at a higher resolution than the CRT display.

Digital plotters produce the highest-quality graphics, and the Hewlett-Packard HP-7470A plotter set a high standard for under-$1000 plotters that was quickly copied by other precision-instrument producers. Plotters operate through relatively simple software interfaces and are capable of multiple color plots. Unlike dot-matrix printers, lines are continuous, not sets of dots, so the overall quality of the plot is higher than a dot-matrix plot.

For some applications, the simplest way to get hard copy of a screen is to take a picture of it. This requires a bit of experimentation, particularly with color, but is fast with an instant camera, requires no special software, and has very high resolution. Special camera hoods and attachments are available for this application.

Finally, computer graphics provide a new dimension to the use of visual stimuli in experiments. The ability of a computer easily to create animated graphics makes it useful when dealing with children (or bored college sophomores); the ability of the machine to display graphics for a precisely determined period of time simplifies the control of psychological experiments in recognition and recall, where timing is critical.

9. ODDS AND ENDS

Communications and Terminal Emulation

With a modem and appropriate software, a PC can be used as a remote terminal to a mainframe computer and transfer text files between computers. The equipment necessary for this is now standard in many machines, including notebook computers.

Modems. A MOdulator-DEModulator converts digital information into a series of tones that are transmitted over a phone line. Until recently, most modems used an "acoustical coupler," which transmitted through the handpiece of a telephone; newer and faster versions plug directly into the phone set. The modem either connects directly into a peripheral slot or uses an RS-232C interface. Most modems operate at 300 baud (roughly 30 characters per second; $100-$200) or 1200 baud (120 cps; $300-$500); 2400 baud modems exist, but they are expensive and function poorly on many standard telephone lines.

All factors being equal, faster modems are preferable. At 300 baud a full 80 × 24 text screen requires a minute to fill, and is considerably slower than reading speed; 1200 baud takes only a quarter of that time. However, in situations in which phone connections are noisy (e.g., long-distance) 300 baud may be preferable because it is more reliable. "Smart" modems with appropriate software can initiate communications automatically, dialing another computer, logging into the system, sending and receiving files, and then logging off and hanging up the phone. Smart modems can also be programmed to answer a phone and receive information. A popular use of this facility is off-hour transmission to lower long-distance charges.

Terminal emulation. With suitable software ($50-$100) a PC can emulate any one of a number of terminals. The simplest task is the emulation of "dumb" terminals; a variety of public-domain programs will do this. Even dumb terminal emulation requires correct matches among program, computer, interface, and receiving computer. Configuration involves correctly setting several parameters in the program. If you don't know where to start, try 300 or 1200 baud (depending on your modem), 8-bit, 1 stop-bit, no parity, and Xon/Xoff. If this doesn't work, experiment until the text in the log-on sequence looks correct. Most systems can be configured with a bit of trial and error, provided the system lets you continue experimenting rather than assuming you are trying to break in.

PCs can also emulate the intelligent terminals used with mainframe programs such as screen editors and graphics displays. Emulation programs are available for most widely used terminals, so a single PC can emulate a variety of terminals in order to match the host system.

File Transfer. File transfers allow information stored on one computer to be transferred to another. For example, the easiest way to transfer a file of text from an IBM to an Apple is to connect the two machines directly, using communications programs, or connect each to a third computer, since the disks are not compatible. File transfers allow work to be shared between a micro and mainframe. For example, in statistical work, exploratory analysis can be done on the PC, then the data set uploaded to use specialized routines available only on a mainframe, or a data set cleaned on a mainframe with downloading for statistical analysis on a PC.

File transfer programs must match the "file protocols" used by the transmitting and receiving computers, particularly when transferring data other than ASCII text. The XMODEM or "Christensen" protocol is commonly used on bulletin boards; the KERMIT protocol is commonly used in academic environments. When downloading files, it is helpful if the PC can send a "stop/resume transmission" signal to the mainframe when saving information to disk; this is usually done by turning on the "Xon/Xoff" facility in the communications program.

Two problems commonly arise in file transfers. First, it is difficult to transfer a file that contains "control characters" (ASCII value less than 32). Some word processors—notoriously WordStar—employ control characters extensively, and these will wreak havoc on many mainframe communications systems. Some communications programs will "trap" incoming or outgoing control characters and convert them to something innocuous (e.g., CTRL-S to ^ S); these characters can later be reconverted with a global replace command in a text editor. The data files of most programs (e.g., spreadsheets, statistical programs) are unintelligible to other computers and programs and must be converted to ASCII text before they are transmitted, then reconverted to data files by the receiving machine.

Installations with a number of computers sometimes connect them with "local area networks" or LANs. LANs work at very high speeds and allow a number of machines to share peripherals such as printers and hard disks. Several totally incompatible LAN protocols exist: "Ethernet" is currently the most popular system and the "Applenet" protocol is popular for connecting Apple equipment.

Voice and Music Synthesis

Voice and music synthesis are well-developed PC applications where dramatic results can be achieved with a minimum of programming.

Newer PCs have very sophisticated voice and music capabilities; old machines require specialized hardware for voice or music.

Voice. Voice synthesizers are relatively inexpensive ($250-$500) and easily programmed with well-developed software. Voice synthesizers employ a combination of preprogrammed common words and phonemes, the basic units of speech. The synthesizer connects to the PC using a standard interface, and text transmitted to the synthesizer is converted to speech under software control.

Existing systems can do a very good rendition of common English language text. A PC can easily read a text file aloud with few mistakes, albeit in a monotone "computer" voice. With additional work, realistic phrasing and intonation can be added; a well-programmed synthesized voice is almost indistinguishable from an electronically amplified human voice.

Voice input is far less well developed. Existing systems can be "trained" to recognize a limited vocabulary (fewer than 100 words) by a single speaker in a clean acoustic environment, but even under these conditions errors are common. Voice recognition is the subject of substantial research since voice is considered preferable to keyboard input for managerial Neanderthals who find keyboards demeaning, and in industrial applications where a keyboard is impractical. Progress has been slow to date.

Music. The status of music is similar to that of voice. Low-quality music hardware is inexpensive (less than $200) and included in some PCs. Higher-quality systems with multiple tone channels cost between $900 and $2000. Music peripheral boards use a conventional stereo amplifier for output and must use a screen editor for input, though more advanced systems use an electronic organ keyboard. The Musical Instrument Digital Interface (MIDI) protocol allows a number of instruments to be played through a single controller.

Analog-Digital Interfacing

Many types of laboratory equipment can be controlled or monitored with analog-to-digital (A/D) input and digital-to-analog (D/A) output interfaces. These convert voltages (analog) to numbers (digital) and vice versa. A/D-D/A boards cost between $90 and $300, depending on the speed and number of channels and other characteristics. With appropriate hardware and software, a number of different devices can be monitored simultaneously by a single PC, information stored on disk, and the printer used as a chart recorder.

Multiple channel control can simplify the design of equipment, since intelligence and coordination can be handled by the PC, rather than built into the equipment. Assembly language programming is usually required to get A/D interfaces working properly. Steve Ciarcia's "Circuit Cellar" column in *Byte* has discussed virtually every type of environmental sensor at one point or another; Ciarcia (1979, 1982) and Uffenbeck (1983) give additional detail. Needless to say, it is helpful to know some electronics before interfacing equipment, to avoid destroying the machine.

While the A/D interface is the most common, there is equipment that uses standard interfaces such as the RS-232C. For example, a camera with an RS-232C interface can use the same peripheral control card as an acoustical modem. Computer-controlled slide projectors, thermometers, pH meters and various sensors are available. The weak point in this area is the present lack of inexpensive, stable, accurate sensors. Considerable progress is being made in the development of these, and a lot can be done by cleverly adapting sensors intended for other uses.

The PC-controlled robot is presently not well developed. The problem, again, is sensors. While it is easy (albeit expensive) to program a robot arm to move a robot hand to a given location, programming that hand to adjust to whether it has picked up a rock or an egg is difficult, as is programming it to find the rock if it has been misplaced slightly. Following Jerry Pournelle's law: "Iron is expensive; silicon is cheap," the first practical robots will, like the first practical printers, be expensive, even if they are intelligent.

Security

The security of information on computers has become an issue in recent years. In general, a computer system is no less secure than any other type of information storage, *if proper precautions are taken!* In fact, a computer system can be much more secure with proper effort. Precautions are at three levels: physical security, passwords, and encryption.

The physical security of disks provides the greatest return for the least amount of effort. People cannot steal or modify what they do not have. Microcomputers are far more secure in this regard than mainframe computers. As long as floppy disks and their backups are in a secure place, you will have no difficulty with security. If a disk is important and difficult to replace, store the backup somewhere remote from the original—fires, floods, and the like sometimes occur. If you've got a disk you want left alone, labels such as "MEMOS" and "1957 AG DEPT

CORN DATA" attract less attention than "C23 GRADE RECORDS" and "MY SECRET DIARY," irrespective of actual disk contents. Keep track of disks so you know if one is missing.

PASSWORDS are increasingly used in microcomputers in systems where there is multiple access to a hard disk and to encrypt files such as spreadsheets that may contain sensitive financial information. Passwords on *floppy* disks offer little protection except against casual intrusion since patch programs used for disk repair can read past any password-protected directory.

On multiple-user systems, passwords provide protection only if they are used properly. The spate of computer "break-ins" in 1982-83 was due to poor practices, such as three-letter passwords and obvious passwords such as SYSTEM, TEST, BLANK, and JONES. Three-letter passwords can be broken by brute force in an average of 23,000 tries, which is simple for a machine programmed to try many combinations a second. A ten-character password, in contrast, requires an average of 2 quadrillion attempts to crack with brute force.

On a password system, don't use obvious passwords such as your name or the name of your car or mate, your favorite four-letter word, or even your mother's maiden name. Be creative. Use long passwords and change them regularly. Use different passwords at different levels of the system—the password used to get into the system should not be the same one used to protect files. Change the password on any file that you've let someone else use. These admonitions apply more to shared systems than to micros, but are worth repeating.

The highest level of security is achieved by enciphering, which can protect a file from all but the most sophisticated attack. Foster (1982) reviews the traditional enciphering methods using a microcomputer approach. These use character-for-character substitution, so an enciphered file will fit in the same space as the original.

For *really* serious enciphering, the recently developed "public key" ciphers are very effective and are virtually unbreakable provided sufficiently long keys are used. These involve long computation time and an expansion of the resulting file by a factor of 1.2 to 1.8. In public key ciphers, knowledge of only the encoding algorithm and key is no help in deciphering, so an individual can encipher information without being able to decipher it. For example, interviewers collecting confidential information could be given an enciphering program and key to encipher the data they collect, but no interviewer would be able to read information collected by others, or even reread his or her own files.

Enciphering is a dangerous tool—if the key is lost, the information is gone. Enciphered files, unlike damaged disks or password-protected systems, cannot be recovered. Enciphering is one step away from lost data. The physical security of the disk is the safest method, and other techniques are best reserved for situations in which physical security cannot be guaranteed.

Repairs

Microcomputers are generally very reliable, but they still occasionally need repair and upgrading. Because the modern PC is primarily composed of off-the-shelf parts, and because PC repair services are usually overworked, overpriced, and often as not incompetent, one should seriously consider doing one's own elementary repairs.

PCs have become considerably more reliable as the number of parts they contain has decreased and manufacturing techniques have been perfected. If a PC survives an initial "burn-in" of about 100 hours, it will probably last for years without major repairs provided it is in a clean, cool environment. I used to spend about $100 a year on my circa-1980 Apple II; in contrast, we've spent only about $40 in two years on repairs on seven Macintoshes in our computer lab, and all of those repairs were for peripherals, not for the computers themselves. However, that $40 could have been $1,000 had we used outside help for simple repairs.

Repairs require appropriate information and parts. Information can be obtained from users' groups, PC magazines, and books (e.g., Brenner, 1985, for the Apple II; similar books exist for the IBM PC and Macintosh). Parts can be obtained from electronics stores—Radio Shack is the ubiquitous favorite—or mail-order sources. Do not expect to get parts, information, or sympathy from your local computer store, as you are taking away a very profitable part of their business.

There are four things to remember. First, user repairs (except on cables) will void the warranty on the machine, though this is irrelevant once the warranty has expired. Second, never work with *power supplies* unless you know exactly what you are doing—these can contain *potentially lethal voltages even when the machine is unplugged!!* You should also exercise extreme care when working near video tubes (e.g., on the Mac). Third, always unplug a PC before working on it. Fourth, chips are extremely sensitive to static electricity, and printed circuit boards are sensitive to heat (e.g., soldering irons), so it is possible to damage a machine if you aren't careful. Start simple and don't attempt a repair you feel uncomfortable with.

That said, the following repairs are common, simple, and highly cost-effective. A couple of screwdrivers, a chip puller and inserter (Radio Shack, about $8), wire cutters, and a soldering iron (for cables) will be sufficient for most repairs.

ROUTINE MAINTENANCE

PCs are almost, but not quite, maintenance free. The few things that do require maintenance can make an otherwise perfectly good machine appear out of order and require an expensive service charge if ignored. Here are three maintenance examples; see the machine's manual for others.

Change fan filters. Some PC fans have filters that must be changed occasionally. With a dirty filter the fan will work inefficiently and the machine may overheat. Changing a filter requires only the new filter and five minutes.

Adjust disk drive speed. Disk drives on older computers such as CP/M machines and early Apple IIs need occasional speed adjustment. If the drives are out of adjustment, they will improperly read and write disks. Utility programs are widely available through commercial and public-domain sources for adjusting disk speed; a small screwdriver and about fifteen minutes will do the job.

Clean the mouse. Mice pick up dust, grease, and lint as they are used. A dirty mouse has a sluggish, unpredictable response to movement. I use a penknife to scrape deposits off the wheels inside the Mac mouse— compare a new mouse with a dirty one to see where grime accumulates. Merely cleaning the ball of the mouse—as the Macintosh manual suggests—does almost nothing.

CABLES

Most cables can be made for less than $10 in parts and with 15 minutes of labor. Some standard cables (e.g., RS232C) are mass produced and cost-effective to buy, but specialized cables (e.g., most Macintosh cables) are overpriced. Radio Shack carries the appropriate plugs and usually the cable (if not, try mail-order); all you need to know are the pin assignments; then you just do a bit of soldering.

CHIP REPLACEMENTS

Cheap 256K memory chips have a fairly high failure rate but are easily replaced provided the chips are in sockets rather than soldered. Most PCs do a memory check when booting and provide a code that identifies the bad chip; otherwise you'll need a program to identify the defective chip. Use a chip puller and inserter, be sure to get the chip inserted in the correct direction, and keep in mind that chips are easily damaged by static. Currently, 256K RAM chips cost about $3 retail; I keep a few in my desk to repair our Macs and IBMs. A $3 chip and 15 minutes will save a $75 repair bill.

If chips other than RAM fail they are more difficult to diagnose and, in the case of proprietary chips, almost impossible to obtain. Here one usually must resort to the repair shop.

INSTALLING PERIPHERALS

Most peripherals such as hard disks and RAM expansion are designed to be installed by the user. Follow the instructions *very* carefully, take your time, and avoid static electricity, and these usually go fine.

CLEANING

Computers can get grimy, particularly if they are in a dusty or smoky environment. Periodic cleaning of contacts on plug-in cards will eliminate a lot of problems—use a pencil eraser to clean off carbon deposits, or an appropriate cleaning solvent. Fans and their filters should be cleaned periodically.

These are the simplest repairs: with proper information and a steady hand, far more complicated repairs and modifications can be done. In 1985, thousands of Macintosh owners upgraded their 128K Macs to 512K by following the instructions published by *Dr. Dobbs Journal*— the do-it-yourself upgrade cost about $100; Apple was charging $800. At those price differentials, one is being paid very well for one's time. Do not attempt repairs without adequate information—PCs cannot be fixed intuitively—but it you've got that information, don't be too intimidated to use it.

10. FINAL THOUGHTS

Buying a Computer

Ownership of a PC is not a necessity of modern living but is attractive on a number of grounds. Having used a PC for some time, you will be in a considerably better position to shop than the complete novice, but keep in mind the following points.

First, compare prices on the *complete* system that you want. Interfaces, software, and peripherals can easily double the cost of a PC. "Bundled" systems, which include interfaces and software, are frequently an excellent deal, though look at what the bundled software will do, not at what the vendor imaginatively claims it would cost. If buying a "compatible" machine, be sure that it works with the software you intend to use. If possible, get the entire setup—PC, peripherals, and software—demonstrated before you buy.

Do not try too hard to save money. A very inexpensive system will probably give disappointing results, and a heavily discounted price means no after-sale service. It is better to wait and buy a good system than prematurely to buy an inadequate one. It is usually better to buy the principal components locally; the motherboard, disk drives, monitor, and keyboard are most likely to need repair. Mail order is the norm on software and unusual peripherals: the dealer will refer you to the manufacturer for repairs and advice anyway, so you might as well get a discount. Never pay list price on software, and rarely on peripherals.

The average user is advised to avoid being the first in the area to own any software or hardware. If you *like* figuring out problems, then explore, but expect problems. On the other hand, don't buy something just because everybody else has it, when reliable information indicates a better or cheaper alternative is available. Word of mouth—friends, users' groups, electronic bulletin boards—is the currency in this business; trade publications (see bibliography) are also helpful. Salespersons, software house hype, and ads usually are not very helpful.

Information for the computer owner is available from a variety of sources. The burgeoning computer-oriented publishing business provides books and periodicals targeting audiences ranging from the least experienced user to the computer professional. PC users' groups exist in many areas, and these are invaluable sources of information, public-domain software, and contacts with individuals using similar hardware and software. Most users' groups are organized around specific hardware, though some exist for complex popular software (e.g., WordStar, Lotus 1-2-3, or dBase II, as well as Zork and Wizardry). Larger users' groups operate on the national electronic bulletin boards of TeleNet, CompuServe, and the Source. National groups are organized around operating systems such as CP/M, MS-DOS, UNIX, and the Macintosh, and languages such as Turbo Pascal. These groups include representatives of the software developers and, as such, are a direct connection to the source of software.

The Future

The PC has come a long way in ten years and promises to go a lot further in the next ten. This section discusses areas where I anticipate the micro will be substantially augmented in the near (5 to 10 year) future. All of the hardware developments are currently available but are not currently part of the common PC.

PCs are approaching true mainframe capabilities in memory and speed. The first personal computers had 16K memory, but now most new machines come with 1 megabyte or more. With costs per byte still dropping and new chips such as the 80386 and 68020 able to address many megabytes, PCs with multimegabyte RAM are clearly in the future. Increased RAM increases the sophistication and speed of programs, particularly in graphics, artificial intelligence, file management, and statistics.

Microprocessor speed has increased by "only" a factor of ten to twenty (initially 1 Mhz; now 16 to 25 Mhz) in contrast to the twenty- to fiftyfold increase in memory (64K; now 1 to 12 Mb) but the increase is quite significant, particularly when it is combined with coprocessors for numerical computing, graphics, and peripherals. The fastest commercially available PCs (e.g., the Levco Prodigy 4 68020/68881-enhanced Macintosh) runs 50% faster than a VAX 11/785 (*Byte* 11, 12: 326), so PCs generally will surpass the speeds of 1986 mainframes in a few more years.

"Floppy" disks have ten times the capacity of those originally introduced, and are now highly reliable. Hard disks with 10 to 50 Mb capacity are now small, reasonable in price, and a standard feature on many newer systems. Optical ROM mass storage in the gigabyte (1,000 Mb) range is now available for very large data sets and reference data bases, though it has not been adopted rapidly in the PC market. A variety of WORM (write-once, read-mostly) optical drives have been introduced, though they are still expensive and experimental.

In all likelihood, future PCs will primarily use visually oriented operating systems and mice, though the huge reservoir of software in the MS-DOS and UNIX operating environments will ensure them a future for some time. Screen resolution will go to about $1,024 \times 1,024$ bytes; resolution beyond that cannot be perceived easily by the eye. LAN protocols are gradually being standardized, as are interface standards such as SCSI, which increase the flexibility of peripherals and reduce their price.

Three peripherals still need developing; a successful, low-cost solution to any will be widely used. Voice recognition is desirable as a supplement to keyboard control, but results thus far have been disappointing—this is a software problem. A text recognition device capable of reading common text fonts with near-perfect accuracy and costing around $1,000 should be available within a couple of years—the necessary parts are available, but some design and software problems remain. Finally, a reliable and inexpensive robot or robot arm would be helpful, particularly if it could provide tactile feedback (e.g., pressure) and some form of sight: Robots are still experimental and expensive.

The implications of this new hardware power are unclear, but it should lead to software that is easy to use while vastly more powerful than anything currently available. There is almost total agreement that software development lags far behind hardware development, and that many of the important software applications have not been developed. PCs have already led to several software breakthroughs that, while conceptually simple, never occurred in the thirty years of mainframe software development: The VisiCalc spreadsheet of Dan Bricklin and Robert Frankston opened a whole new business programming genre; Nolan Bushnell's Pong set off a multibillion-dollar video games industry; Bill Atkinson's MacPaint brought graphics editing off the $30,000 graphics work stations and into the 128K Macintosh, paving the way for desktop publishing.

Two trends characterize contemporary software development. The first is the development and standardization of "operating environments" that allow a programmer to utilize a large set of preprogrammed tools. Both the Macintosh operating system and UNIX are examples of this. An operating environment has two advantages. First, programs become more powerful because a small program can invoke thousands of lines of supporting tool code. Second, because the same tools are used in a variety of programs, different programs written by different companies still have much in common and are consequently easier to learn. Of course, there is a cost to the programmer in learning those tools: For example, in 1985 it was generally estimated that a commercial Macintosh program took about six more months to write than a comparable MS-DOS program, though this differential has diminished somewhat.

Second, programs are becoming more intelligent in the sense of being more able to react to, adapt to, and anticipate the needs of the user. Some of this intelligence is achieved through formal artificial intelligence techniques such as expert systems; additional "intelligence" is obtained by sophisticated interfaces that incorporate error checking and provide appropriate help when asked. Most Macintosh software can be used almost to full capacity without ever opening the manual, which would have been unthinkable in a mainframe or CP/M system. This reduces the time and effort involved in learning to use any program, and thus increases the likelihood that a program will be used.

Software development is still an art and not a science, and may remain so indefinitely. Software development is labor intensive rather than capital intensive. In innovative programming, an individual working alone at home can still outperform a corporation, particularly when the application is new. Most successful PC software firms were started by individuals, not spun off Fortune 500 companies. The decentralization of both software development and marketing probably means that more labor-hours of programming will be spent on academic PC software in the 1980s than were spent on academic mainframe software during the 30 years before 1980. With PC approaching mainframe capabilities, and software simultaneously become more powerful and easier to use, the future looks bright.

BIBLIOGRAPHY

Periodicals

Berkeley Macintosh Users' Group. This group publishes a fantastic semi-annual magazine and is a splendid source of information on Macintosh computing in an academic environment. Open to anybody, not just UC Berkeley (1442A Walnut St., #2, Berkeley, CA 94709; phone 415-849-9114; call for current membership rates).

Byte. One of the first microcomputer periodicals, *Byte* is virtually the journal of record for the field. It is technical, somewhat hardware oriented, and probably heavy going for a beginner. However, everything sooner or later ends up in *Byte* (P.O. Box 328, Hancock, NH 03449; $21/yr).

Computer Language. This is a fairly new magazine aimed at programmers; it is a good source of algorithms, compiler benchmarks, and programming techniques. An associated magazine, *AI/Expert*, focuses on artificial intelligence (P.O. Box 10953, Palo Alto, CA 94303-0967; $29.95 per year).

InfoWorld. A newsweekly known for up-to-date information on the microcomputer industry, frequent and competent product reviews; takes itself considerably less seriously than most. Aimed at the industry as a whole (375 Cochituate Road, Framingham, MA 01701; $31/yr).

Social Science Micro Review. Currently the only publication devoted exclusively to social science computing. Quarterly (Duke University Press, Periodicals Dept., 6697 College Station, Durham, NC 27708; phone 919-684-2173; $24/yr).

Note Regarding Machine-Specific Magazines: There are a number of magazines aimed at specific PCs (e.g., Apple II, IBM PC, Atari, Macintosh) available at mass-market bookstores (and 7-11 Stores, for that matter). They have the life expectancy of gerbils: Last time

I recommended one it went out of business before the book was printed. Browse and buy a couple until you find which ones are useful.

Books

BARR, A., P. R. COHEN, and E. A. FEIGENBAUM [eds.] (1981-1982) *Handbook of Artificial Intelligence*, vols. 1-3. New York: Basic Books.
Encyclopedic coverage of the state of the art in AI; definitely not a beginners' text but a good reference work.

BRENNER, R. (1984) *Apple II Plus/IIe Troubleshooting and Repair Guide*. Indianapolis: Howard W. Sams & Company.
Much of the book is specific to the Apple, but it is an excellent beginners' guide to repairing computers.

CIARCIA, S. (1979-1982) *Ciarcia's Circuit Cellar*, 3 vols. New York: McGraw-Hill.
Collections of Ciarcia's articles from *Byte* that have dealt with almost every conceivable electronic device for PCs, up to and including an entire computer. Particularly good on sensors and interfaces.

CLOCKSIN, W. and C. MELLISH (1981) *Programming in Prolog*. New York: Springer-Verlag.
The original document defining Prolog, though subsequent implementations (e.g., Turbo Prolog) frequently deviate significantly from it.

FOLEY, J. D. and A. VAN DAM (1982) *Fundamentals of Interactive Computer Graphics*. Reading, MA: Addison-Wesley.
Comprehensive reference text on graphics.

FOSTER, C. C. (1982) *Cryptanalysis for Microcomputers*. Rochelle Park, NJ: Hayden.
A primer on cipher systems up to, but not including, the recent public key ciphers.

GONNET, G. (1984) *Handbook of Algorithms and Data Structures*. Reading, MA: Addison-Wesley.
Just what it says—a useful reference work for programmers.

JENSEN, K. and N. WIRTH (1978) *Pascal User Manual and Report*. New York: Springer-Verlag.
The ultimate reference on standard Pascal—a technical document vital for reference but not a book from which to learn the language.

KERNIGHAN, B. W. and P. J. PLAUGER (1981) *Software Tools in Pascal*. Reading, MA: Addison-Wesley.
General collection of routines for text and file processing. Originally translated out of FORTRAN so could presumably be easily translated back into BASIC.

KERNIGHAN, B. W. and D. M. RITCHIE (1978) *The C Programming Language*. Englewood Cliffs, NJ: Prentice-Hall.
The definitive reference work on C—both defines the language and provides a programming tutorial.

KIDDER, T. (1982) *Soul of a New Machine.* New York: Avon.
The single best journalistic account of the computer profession, centering on the development of a new microcomputer.

KNUTH, D. (1980) *The Art of Computer Programming,* 3 vols. Reading, MA: Addison-Wesley.
An encyclopedia of algorithms for all phases of computer science. A comprehensive but difficult work, at the level of a graduate mathematics text, but considerably lightened by Knuth's humor.

KOCHAN, S. and P. WOOD (1984) *Exploring the UNIX System.* Hasbrouck Heights, NJ: Hayden.
Good, readable introduction to UNIX.

LANDRETH, B. (1985) *Out of the Inner Circle: A Hacker's Guide to Computer Security.* Bellevue, WA: Microsoft Press.
A good demystification of hacking.

LUEHRMANN, A. and H. PECKHAM (1981) *Apple Pascal: A Hands-On Approach.* New York: McGraw-Hill.
It should be possible to learn Pascal from this book alone, provided you work through all the exercises. With some variations it applies to any UCSD p-System computer, not just Apple.

McGILTON, H. and R. MORGAN (1983) *Introducing the UNIX System.* New York: McGraw-Hill.
Just what it says—general, text-level introduction.

REMER, D. (1982) *Legal Care for Your Software.* Reading, MA: Addison-Wesley.
If you happen to write something that might sell, this is a handy book to have around.

RUCKDESCHEL, F. R. (1981) *BASIC Scientific Subroutines.* New York: McGraw-Hill.
A good reference on basic algorithms for numerical work. Two volumes; Volume 2 contains most of the numerical material.

UFFENBECK, J. E. (1983) *Hardware Interfacing with the Apple II Plus.* Englewood Cliffs, NJ: Prentice-Hall.
General introduction with thirteen experiments, including A/D and D/A interfaces. Uffenbeck has written a comparable text for the TRS-80.

WINSTON, P. (1984) *Artificial Intelligence.* Reading, MA: Addison-Wesley.
A general introductory survey of the field; relatively nontechnical and designed as a textbook.

WINSTON, P. and B. HORN (1984) *LISP.* Reading, MA: Addison-Wesley.
Second edition of the classic textbook on LISP, focusing on the "Common LISP" dialect.

Note Regarding Assembly Language Programming: Assembly programming is considerably more difficult to learn than either BASIC or Pascal, though numerous books are available. Browse, but be sure to find a book that corresponds *exactly* to the machine on which you are planning to learn; otherwise you will be hopelessly lost.

Note Regarding Popular Computer Books: I have not listed here popular introductions to the IBM PC, MS-DOS, the Macintosh, WordStar, Excel, BASIC, and so forth. Mass-market bookstores such as Barnes and Noble, B. Dalton, and Waldenbooks carry a large number of these books, particularly in stores in business districts. Many such books are of high quality, others are junk; all have a short half-life because the systems they describe change rapidly. For that same reason, libraries are almost useless as a source of PC books: By the time a book is ordered and catalogued, it is probably outdated. Browse the shelves of bookstores looking for books that correspond to the version of the software or hardware you are trying to understand, have a recent copyright date, and seem intelligible. A good book can save hours of time and is well worth the investment.

PHILIP A. SCHRODT is Associate Professor of Political Science at Northwestern University, where he also teaches in the Mathematical Methods in the Social Sciences Program. He holds an M.A. in mathematics from Indiana University in addition to a Ph.D. in political science, and has taught computer programming since 1970. Dr. Schrodt's primary research interests are mathematical models of political behavior, with a focus on international relations; he has also developed commercial software for the Apple II computer.